Introduction

Welcome to the *New York Times Thursday Crossword Book.* You will find herein one hundred puzzles, edited by the legendary Eugene T. Maleska, all of which originally appeared in the pages of *The New York Times* on Thursdays.

The *Times* crosswords have traditionally increased in difficulty through the week, with Monday's puzzle meant to get your week started on a confident note, and Saturdays, worked on by most people at home, meant to provide a substantial mental workout. By introducing this new series of *Times* crosswords grouped by the day of the week, it is our hope that puzzlers of every skill will find the book that is just right for them.

This book of Thursday crosswords, slightly more difficult than Wednesday's, rates about a "6" on the toughness scale, with Monday being a "1" and Saturday being a "10."

Best wishes for happy puzzling!

Stanley Newman
Managing Director,
Puzzles & Games

W9-AYV-146

Published by Ivy Books:

THE NEW YORK TIMES DAILY CROSSWORD PUZZLES—
MONDAY

THE NEW YORK TIMES DAILY CROSSWORD PUZZLES—
TUESDAY

THE NEW YORK TIMES DAILY CROSSWORD PUZZLES—
WEDNESDAY

THE NEW YORK TIMES DAILY CROSSWORD PUZZLES—
THURSDAY

THE NEW YORK TIMES DAILY CROSSWORD PUZZLES—
FRIDAY

THE NEW YORK TIMES DAILY CROSSWORD PUZZLES—
SATURDAY

THE
NEW YORK TIMES
DAILY CROSSWORD
PUZZLES

THURSDAY

VOLUME 1

Edited by
Eugene T. Maleska

IVY BOOKS • NEW YORK

An Ivy Book
Published by The Random House Publishing Group
Copyright © 1997 by Random House, Inc.

Published in the United States by Ivy Books, an imprint of The Random House Publishing Group, a division of Random House, Inc., New York, and simultaneously in Canada by Random House of Canada Limited, Toronto.

Ivy and colophon are trademarks of Random House, Inc.

All of the puzzles that appear in this work were originally published in *The New York Times* Thursday editions from January 1, 1987, through December 24, 1988. Copyright © 1987, 1988 by The New York Times Company. All Rights Reserved. Reprinted by permission.

www.ballantinebooks.com

ISBN 0-8041-1582-6

Text design and typography by Mark Frnka

Printed in Canada

First Edition: February 1997

19 18 17 16 15 14

THE
NEW YORK TIMES
DAILY CROSSWORD
PUZZLES

THURSDAY

VOLUME 1

ACROSS

1 Pharm. watchdog
4 Groups of rioters
8 Drive back
13 Miscellany
14 In __ (stagnant)
15 "Give __ man thy ear . . .": Shak.
16 Prophetess without honor
18 Baseball great
19 Lived dangerously
21 Softly, in Sonora
22 Cashiers
23 Grossglockner, e.g.
25 Crescent-shaped part, formerly
27 Crew
31 Father of Abner
32 Quote
33 The world according to Arp
34 Lived dangerously
38 Forge implement
39 Kick
40 Choose
41 Beheld
42 City on the Elbe
44 Western lizard
45 Bouquet __ (chef's bunch of herbs)
47 Pitcher Nolan __
50 Lived dangerously
56 Of a cubitus
57 Volatile
58 Spokes
59 Control
60 Killer whales
61 __ Gay, W.W. II plane
62 Inquires, in Dogpatch
63 Half of an African fly

DOWN

1 Criticism
2 View unfavorably
3 N Italian city
4 Lute's cousin
5 Church calendar
6 Live dangerously
7 Nike or Venus, e.g.
8 Send payment
9 Site of Northwestern U.
10 Graceful girl
11 __ Blair (George Orwell)
12 Defervesce
13 School for would-be Lts.
17 Dem. leader in the 50's
20 Presidential monogram
23 Pilasters
24 Former Italian president

2

26 All-purpose trk.
28 Meets
29 Maven
30 River of Thrace
32 Mountain pass
33 Welcome __
35 Long-billed bird
36 Peruse
37 Makes raucous
42 Grand __,
   Evangeline's
   home

43 A memorable
   Gandhi
46 Heart chambers
48 Cries of contempt
49 Neckwear
50 Salt or smoke
51 Pearl Buck heroine
52 Ruin
53 Any letter in NATO
54 Suffix with depend
55 Some coll.
   linemen

ACROSS

1 Piece of cake
6 A symbol of Eire
10 Nashville university
14 Authorized
15 Melville novel
16 Fainéant
17 Montemezzi's "L'__ dei Tre Re"
18 Pulitzer Prize dramatist: 1927
20 Boat basin
22 Emulated Rosalynn Sumners
23 Famed Green Bay Packer
26 Cheers for the above
29 Items of interest to realtors
30 Jazz style
34 Rhea's cousin
35 Othello, for one
36 Take off
37 Site of Pago Pago
39 London suburb
41 Sand ridge
42 Hokkaido city
43 Bound
45 Do wrong
46 Belgrade coin
47 Rose Bowl champs: 1986
48 Highfalutin'
49 Greenhorns
52 City ENE of Nantes
54 Enfold
58 Site of Cape Farewell
61 Flynn of filmdom
62 Seaweed derivative
63 Hodgepodge
64 Athens attraction
65 Colorful parrot
66 Sheet of stamps
67 Kipling's word for "a good cigar"

DOWN

1 Coup in bridge
2 Champagne Tony of golf
3 Borodin's prince
4 West Indian group
5 Diva Obraztsova
6 Poe's "__-Frog"
7 Candlenut
8 Drives out
9 Strenuous dance
10 Evergreens
11 __ fixe
12 Vehicle for Frome
13 Range of knowledge
19 Mixed up
21 Guthrie
24 Stole
25 Indulge in pandiculation
26 Do a lawn job
27 Violin maker
28 "The __ Comedy": Saroyan

4

31 Napoleon creator
32 Public
33 He "opened" Japan: 1854
35 Actress O'Hara
38 Type of greenhouse
40 Like a coyote
44 Chophouse sign
47 N.J. college
48 Flavoring agent from ginger
50 Warship deck

51 Urns
52 Former constellation
53 Contiguous
55 The Andrews Sisters, e.g.
56 Brant's sound
57 In addition
58 Unit of acceleration
59 "Winter of Artifice" author
60 Bambi's dam

ACROSS

1 Bex and Dax
5 Hi, in Hilo
10 Baker-Charlie precursor
14 Expletive
15 Recorder
16 Type of deck
17 Pirate
19 Sit
20 Rose-arbor structure
21 Chemist's measurer
23 Freight unit
24 Meat for noisettes
25 Castoffs
29 Cash in on an investment
32 Bridge master Sharif
33 Developers' interests
35 Cicatrix
36 Flick
37 Make a knight
38 Kith's companion
39 Wearers of teeth
41 Sire
43 Rouge et Noire
44 Parliamentary events
46 Minnelli-Grey film
48 Imperfect circle
49 Thrash
50 Russian vehicles
53 Waltz king
57 Pictorial presswork
58 Speakeasy supplier
60 Topping
61 Pop song of Pop's day
62 Radius neighbor
63 Weems and Williams
64 Sounds from a pride
65 Eyots

DOWN

1 Flabby
2 Skegger
3 Fit to __
4 Cover
5 Oils, ecclesiastically
6 French battle site: 1915
7 Polo Grounds hero
8 Dickens villain
9 Gets to Kennedy
10 A court
11 Subservient one
12 Misplaced
13 Foil's relative
18 Common-interest group
22 Coal size
25 Bound
26 Sociologist Durkheim
27 Shod like some fishermen

28 A dodecahedron has 12
29 Ancient instrument
30 Kinshasa is its capital
31 Sculptor-playwright Barlach
34 Pull hard
40 Redeemers
41 Excoriate verbally
42 Squeals

43 Nicaragua's capital
45 "We'll __ a cup . . .": Burns
47 Uncover
50 Pony
51 Spatiate
52 Unaccompanied
53 Ado
54 Jamaican fruit
55 Mailed
56 Madrid Mmes.
59 Harem room

ACROSS

1 Trevino, Watson et al.
5 Wading bird
10 Sunday event for some
14 Goddess of youth
15 Baseball's Big or Little Poison
16 Writer Wiesel
17 Via's kin
18 Get on a soapbox
19 Certain facts
20 Tell it as it is
23 Bean and Welles
24 Medical suffix
25 Rock star
28 Moss Hart autobiography
32 Short haircut
35 Part of 45 Across
37 __ apple
40 Mongrel
41 Brought to bay
42 "It's Too Late" singing star
45 White House monogram
46 Certain laughers
47 Pentateuch
50 Numeric prefix
52 Eats away
56 Treat
60 Unruffled
61 Island in the Firth of Clyde

62 Porridge pot
63 "Battle Hymn . . ." composer
64 Della from Detroit
65 Maine, e.g., to Pierre
66 Word of regret
67 Seaport in S Sweden
68 Blind follower

DOWN

1 Van Dine's Vance
2 Do a new paving job
3 Carries out
4 Comics like Chaplin
5 Actress Kurtz
6 Mountain lake
7 __ the beginning
8 River in Hades
9 Surgeon of a kind
10 Intercessor
11 Pres. Arthur's middle name
12 Place
13 Coral or Red
21 Blaster's material
22 Illumination, in Bonn
26 Sleuth Carter
27 Astronaut's garment
29 Was indebted
30 Poverty
31 Ground, in Berlin

32 One of the B's
33 Singer Anita
34 Uncovered
36 Cube inventor Rubik
38 Glasses not worn by the masses
39 Not taut
43 Sea arm
44 Made verdant
48 Part of a circle
49 Emulated Santa

51 After, in Arles
53 Fourth Greek letter
54 Ostentatious display
55 Ape Hans Brinker
56 Anagram for loop
57 Hawkeye State
58 Waste allowance
59 "Every cloud __ silver . . ."
60 Half of a dance

ACROSS

1 Let
6 Bit of news
10 Money in Ankara
14 First name of a singer from Middlesex
15 Gershwin's "__, Lucille"
16 Suffixes with czar and signor
17 Food fish
18 Essex lover
20 Organic pigments
22 Chat
23 Very much
25 Jelly Roll __, jazz pianist
26 False friend of Ben-Hur
29 Capital of Yemen
30 Crumb
31 __ deaf ear
33 States, in Savoie
37 He kids you not
39 Grand backer
41 Where Perry won: 1813
42 To eat, in Bonn
44 Pluto, to Plato
46 Lass in a Brandon Thomas play
47 Fete
49 Ceremonies
51 Greeting
54 An ophidian
55 Strike __ (equalize)
57 Captivate
61 Mrs. Ferraro
63 Of dreams: Comb. form
64 Winged
65 Envelope abbr.
66 Patron saint of the lame
67 Headland
68 Financial ctr.
69 Astronaut Ride

DOWN

1 So that . . . not
2 Admiral Zumwalt
3 Disk deified by Amenhotep IV
4 Platform makers
5 Plead
6 __ de Ré
7 Powders
8 Bruce of N.F.L. fame
9 Bread or cabbage
10 Free
11 Sluggish
12 Proportion
13 Pale
19 Unisonally
21 Health, to Hadrian
24 Flotow opera
26 Be listless
27 Ages
28 Deps.

10

1	2	3	4	5		6	7	8	9		10	11	12	13
14						15					16			
17						18			19					
20				21		22								
			23		24			25						
26	27	28					29							
30				31			32			33		34	35	36
37			38		39				40		41			
42				43		44				45		46		
			47		48			49			50			
51	52	53					54							
55					56				57			58	59	60
61						62		63						
64				65					66					
67				68					69					

29 Jurist __ Day O'Connor

32 Monogram of a noted astronaut

34 Region

35 Box for bucks

36 Legendary septet

38 Career soldiers

40 Melt the frost

43 Brazilian port

45 Office workers, for short

48 __ ear (listen)

50 Muse of astronomy

51 Scientist Carl __

52 White poplar

53 "__ Theme," from "Doctor Zhivago"

54 Schisms

56 Kind of slicker

58 Factory

59 Pitcher Hershiser

60 Reddish

62 Chemical suffix

ACROSS

1 Brewer's preparation
5 Diving-bell inventor
9 Padnag
14 City N of the Skagerrak
15 Source of some grease
16 Sound
17 Pecan pith
18 Aspen, for one
19 Notched, as a leaf
20 The Great Emancipator
23 "I Was the __," Presley hit
24 Baton Rouge inst.
25 __ Prés, Flemish composer
26 Where Booth struck: April 14, 1865
32 Ostrich's kin
33 Long period
34 Finnish bath
38 Poet Edward Rowland __
40 Passover feast
43 Like a bug in a rug
44 Pass imperceptibly
46 What video means
48 Mrs. Cantor
49 Epithet for 20 Across
53 Rowan
56 Annoy
57 Ripen
58 The Little Giant
64 Hawkins or Thompson
65 Fine feathers
66 Fibber
68 Orchard pest
69 Oil-producing org.
70 White-tailed sea bird
71 Wee
72 Hudson contemporary
73 Willis of N.B.A. fame

DOWN

1 Apple-pie maker
2 Where Shaftoe is
3 Gooden's plate
4 Dragster
5 Art lovers
6 Emanation
7 Form an opinion
8 Kim Hunter role
9 Approaches
10 Painter Chagall
11 Kind of bank or test
12 Thread type
13 British noble family
21 Amphora adjunct
22 Adherent
26 Actor Parker
27 Leave out
28 Principle
29 Gardener's need
30 ". . . __ not yet": Matt. 24:6

12

31 Ethiopian prince
35 Single quantity
36 Like Lady Godiva
37 Culture medium
39 Gibbon
41 Mae West's "Life, Sex and __"
42 Send up another rocket
45 Covered with foam
47 Scottish island
50 Where Dub. is

51 Lady Bird's spouse
52 A job O. Henry had
53 Plus factor
54 Booth's milieu
55 Protect a bet
59 Yaws (the disease)
60 An amino acid
61 Is in debt
62 Yorkshire river
63 Rational
67 Carmine

ACROSS

1 Cookies
6 "__ the Great," Dumm cartoon
10 Campus in Dallas, Tex.
13 Leg bone
14 Prepares to plaster
16 Kind of end or team
17 __ provocateur
18 Look forward to
19 Like Abner
20 Spot for some sun worshipers
23 Exist
24 Till
25 Elements
32 Miss Piggy, to Miss Piggy
33 Ornament
34 Former spouses
36 Outstanding person
38 An area of Italy
39 "Give a man a horse __ ride"
40 Snicker- __
41 Cake, in Madrid
43 Suffix with cook or rook
44 Apt anagram for 25 Across
48 Preacher __, ex-pitcher
49 Author Deighton
50 Apt anagram for 20 Across

59 Act like a human
60 Conform
61 Snow, in Savoie
62 Kind of roll
63 Fits of pique
64 Begin
65 Archil or puccoon
66 Polish partner
67 Solid: Comb. form

DOWN

1 Datum, for short
2 Almost
3 Busy as __
4 Of part of the ear
5 "Juke Box __ Night"
6 Jai __
7 Concerns of judges
8 Utah, to René
9 Arty
10 Norman battle site
11 Chief
12 Surly
15 Seat at a bar
21 __ Sea (part of Jordan's boundary)
22 White House reception
25 Progress
26 Houston N.F.L. player
27 "Theirs __ reason why": Tennyson
28 Nonsense
29 Bergen's Mortimer

14

30 Shine
31 Rises high
32 Hosp. workers
35 Shipbuilder's concern
37 Hear
39 __ hands full (be pressed)
42 Tattle
45 "__ a Stranger": Thompson
46 Condescends

47 Aim
50 Penury
51 Wild time
52 Yen
53 Nerd
54 Asian Bigfoot
55 "__ la guerre"
56 Kathy __, pro golfer
57 Historic Hungarian city
58 Parched

ACROSS

1 Wedels
5 TV's Barnaby Jones
10 Prefix for graph or medic
14 Fraction
15 Ravel's "La __"
16 Arabian cloaks
17 Discomfort
19 City in Calif.
20 Predetermined
21 Muse of comedy
23 Pop's brother
24 Whodunit finale
26 Brutes
30 Heaps
31 Informed
32 Hippodrome
34 Lennon's "__ Do You Sleep?"
37 Singer Orlando
38 Smart
39 Feast
40 Ancient times, to Poe
41 Loyal
42 Because
43 "Die Fledermaus" maid
45 Hurt
47 Animates
50 Immie's kin
51 Dried grape
52 Made-to-order
57 City SE of Belgrade
58 Ornate fixture
60 Egyptian dancer
61 Chalet features
62 Arctic abode
63 Lip
64 Clark role
65 Dramatis personae

DOWN

1 Garden tool
2 Batman's creator
3 Angers
4 Branch of sculpture
5 Manifest
6 Ruination
7 Luges
8 Ar chaser
9 Chick
10 Sense of taste
11 Action demanded by W.L. Garrison
12 Ham's companion
13 Indian, e.g.
18 Burn slightly
22 __ hoop
25 Unlocked
26 Glut
27 Truant G.I.
28 Malicious defacements
29 Soft fabric

16

33 Trucker's wheels
35 Former
36 Dock or knawel
38 Hit man's purchase
39 Fiendish
41 Manufacturer Strauss
42 Show friendship
44 Cookbook contents
46 Surrounded by

47 Soprano Berger et al.
48 Waltz composition by Delibes
49 Keg part
53 Dill of yore
54 Baltic port
55 Lampreys
56 French hurdles champ
59 Cry of triumph

ACROSS

1 Beersheba's locale
6 Behold, to Brutus
10 Panic
14 "A robin redbreast in __": Blake
15 "If __ My Way," 1913 song
16 Bugbear
17 Parkman's Italian cookbook?
20 Sun
21 Road: Ger.
22 Pass on
23 Forfeited
24 Large ratites
26 Eschews hot-dog garnish?
32 Le __, Parisian journal
33 First Earl of Chatham
34 Route
35 Black birds
36 Thrash
38 Middleweight champ: 1941–47
39 Trp. member
40 Up __ good
41 Feeling ennui
42 Busy chef's ironic lament?
46 Bone: Comb. form
47 A daughter of Eurytus
48 Graph

51 Cooler, for some
52 African hemp
55 Dangerous entree at a Greek deli?
59 "Topaz" author
60 Tennyson character
61 Maestro Georg
62 Buck or bull, e.g.
63 Winnows
64 Rembrandt's "Three __"

DOWN

1 One-time D.C. team
2 Canyon phenomenon
3 Celt
4 Conceit
5 Prolix
6 Octave
7 Oland role
8 Put up
9 Tokyo, once
10 Weald
11 Equal, in Arles
12 "Mi chiamano Mimi," e.g.
13 Depend
18 Shrine Bowl team
19 Confidence
23 Some trains: Abbr.
24 Radiate
25 Violin attachment
26 Sea mollusk
27 Solidarity
28 Certain salts

29	Trophy	45	Target on the green
30	Breathing sounds	48	Buddy
31	Stained	49	Olympian figure
32	Part of a derrick	50	See 40 Down
36	To __ (besides)	51	Invent
37	Bancroft or Meara	52	Otiose
38	Torrid or Temperate	53	Honor, in a way
40	Seed coat	54	A sister of Ares
41	Stabilize	56	Ship-shaped clock
43	Gloomy	57	Hereditary letters
44	Gives way	58	And not

ACROSS

1 Cavils
6 Corvine sound
9 Kind of door
13 N.Y. city
14 Turkish title
15 Israeli dance
16 Italian poet
17 Protector of the public
20 Exact by way of levy
22 Adds a glossy coating
23 A deck
25 R.E. Lee's cause
26 Abbr. after a list
29 Bouquets
31 Diving bird
34 Protector of the public
36 Prepare to ride again
38 Tibetan priests
39 Dep.
40 Geological seam, in Sedan
41 Russian composer's family
43 Comics hero
44 W.H.A. contemporary
45 Bacterium needing oxygen
47 Wide shoes
48 __ generis (unique)
49 Coin for René
51 Affront, in Asti
55 Ape
59 Protector of the public
61 ESP word
62 To me, in Tours
63 Dumbbell
64 Blessed __
65 Dir. at sea
66 Asner and Sullivan
67 Snuggeries

DOWN

1 Penal __
2 Word of woe
3 Tear
4 Protector of the public
5 Look of derision
6 Hercules, to Iole
7 In the past
8 Lashing aftermath
9 Unit of discourse
10 "Tony __," Sinatra film
11 Inland sea
12 Slates
18 Peruvian group
19 Tapioca source
21 Ladd of films
24 __ call (where ships stop briefly)
26 Musical key
27 Structural units

28 Actress Anouk
30 __ culpa
31 ". . . can you spare __?"
32 Forearm bones
33 Wails
35 Invasion
37 Protector of the public
39 Leb. neighbor
42 Former Mali statesman

43 Show delight
46 Abridgements
48 Girl in a song
50 Actor David
51 "__ Dream . . ."
52 Alaskan city
53 Uppity one
54 Hautboy
56 Lincoln's namesakes
57 Yurt, e.g.
58 Superlative endings
60 Stripling

ACROSS

1 Roe producer
5 Edison contemporary
10 Small ice mass
14 Douglas Hyde's land
15 Gulae
16 Mishmash
17 Charity
18 Natural disaster
20 Abhorrence
22 Blasphemes
23 Beam
24 Fanfare
26 Artist Bellows: 1882–1925
28 Raised
32 Color again
33 Kringle
35 Réunion, e.g.
36 Common connectors
37 "The Lost __"
38 Baal, for one
39 To's partner
40 Chanticleer's milieu
41 Brazilian territory
42 Stretchable
44 Taste
46 Despots
48 Nitwit
49 Sharpness
52 Turncoats
56 Fault in Calif.
58 Maumee Bay feeder
59 Mix
60 Weird
61 Hawaii's state bird
62 Like quidnuncs
63 Rips
64 Sounds of disapproval

DOWN

1 Official stamp
2 Hawaiian city
3 Decisive battle
4 Wipes out
5 Carpenter's activity
6 Alaskan statesman
7 Where lint may glint
8 Diminutive suffix
9 Mount St. Helens product
10 Woos
11 "__! poor Yorick"
12 Simile word
13 Montcalm and Wolfe, e.g.
19 Seine sights
21 Engage
25 Plots a course
26 Kind or type
27 Copycat

22

29	High walls of water	**43**	Crèche figure
30	Leave with a lover	**45**	Degrades
31	Poet Walter __ Mare	**47**	Opposite of stem
		49	Org.
32	Kon-Tiki, e.g.	**50**	Clouseau's servant
34	__ Alamos		
37	Drainer	**51**	Les États-__
38	Powerless	**53**	Incursion
40	Anagram for serin	**54**	Glaciarium
41	Mine, to Miss Piggy	**55**	Bishoprics
		57	Female ruff

ACROSS

1 Whimper's alternative, at world's end
5 Smelting dross
9 Facilitate
14 Tribe in "The Time Machine"
15 Greeting in the barrio
16 Words on a Wonderland cake
17 Pop
18 Source
19 Grass type
20 Song for a spaced-out batter?
23 Shade of blue
24 Function
25 Sully
28 Browning's Vogler
29 Jannings of "The Blue Angel"
33 Incommunicado
34 Mine, in Metz
35 Cakes' literary partner
36 Song for a misguided tsetse?
40 Thread: Comb. form
41 Billy __, rock singer
42 __-les-Bains, French spa
43 Flanders flower
45 Nice drink
46 __ Buck, 1985 Derby winner
47 Help a hood
49 Flatterer of a sort
50 Song for a happy duck?
57 Dostoyevsky's Myshkin, e.g.
58 Politician's plea
59 Capable of
60 Less
61 "Cielo __!," Ponchielli aria
62 Apollo's mother
63 Like an Irish bog
64 Desiccated
65 Nebraskan Senator

DOWN

1 Harry's wife
2 In the hold, asea
3 Knotty situations
4 Big name in West Coast banking
5 Pardon
6 Wacko
7 Like a bump on __
8 Jacksonville scene of action
9 "Love Story" author
10 A Zoroastrian
11 Coup d'__
12 Madame Bovary
13 "__ Me," Ustinov autobiography
21 Greek physician
22 "Tell it __ Gath"
25 Bonkers
26 Sex psychologist Havelock
27 Morley's Kitty

24

28 Start of an O'Neill
title
30 San Quentin's county
31 Homeric work
32 Soprano Mitchell
34 Coloring agents, e.g.
37 Specified, as a date
38 Hogan's kin
39 Reverse a court
decision
44 Spicy stew
46 Field of activity

48 Itsy-__
49 Rose distillation
50 Chump
51 ". . . mortal or
immortal, here __":
Melville
52 Actress Foch
53 Gold-rush center:
1900
54 Top
55 "Tell __ the Marines!"
56 High time

ACROSS

1 Main artery
6 __ Boleyn
10 Military group
14 Abolitionist-martyr
15 Nun or spar
16 Like the Texas star
17 Statesman Henry __: 1850–1924
19 Galba's garb
20 College activist org.
21 Seek's companion
22 Slave leader: 1800–31
24 Used a loom
25 "My kingdom __ horse!"
26 This goes with the grain
29 Betty Ford's kin
33 Indeed
34 Hialeah hustler
35 Elide
36 Rhyme scheme
37 Abolitionist Sojourner __
38 British seaside tract
39 Kind of club
40 Emerald Isle
41 Compact
42 Abolitionist-editor
44 Henry M. Robert's concern
45 Pool shark Minnesota __
46 Cold-shoulder
48 H.H. Jackson heroine: 1884

51 Victory: Ger.
52 Sydney's state: Abbr.
55 Skunk's defense
56 Create a mosaic
59 Word with brake or jockey
60 Mel and Ed of baseball
61 Starwort
62 Diminutive suffix
63 Optimistic
64 Abolitionist-author

DOWN

1 Kindergarten subj.
2 Direction of a buss
3 Hijacks
4 Company
5 Abolitionist suffragette
6 Manse or condo
7 Duchamp's staircase descender
8 Yule libation
9 Fang
10 Avant-garde
11 Midday
12 The Gloomy Dean: 1860–1954
13 Lachryma
18 Actress Ullmann
23 Tail: Comb. form
24 Abolitionist in England
25 Galway's instrument
26 Famed football coach
27 Musical syllables

28 "Fra Diavolo" composer
29 Brook
30 Correct, in a way
31 Washer cycle
32 Hamburger source
34 Gatlin Brothers et al.
37 His will is his way
41 Lincoln- __ debates
43 Fleming or Hunter
46 Milksop

47 Tee follower
48 Used a buckboard
49 This may lead to lead
50 More than more
51 J.F.K. speedsters
52 Treaty gp.
53 Ragout
54 Sergeant's "As you __!"
57 D.D.E.'s command
58 Amphib. vessel

ACROSS

1 Powdered starches
6 Mineral spring
9 Masters winner: 1957
13 Memorable pianist Oscar __
14 "Le Coq __": Rimsky-Korsakov
15 __ code
16 Masters winner: 1967
17 Grapevine blight, also called black measles
19 Six-time Masters winner
21 Type of fountain
22 Unpaid debts
26 Paley's network
29 Bridge bldr.
31 J. __ Thurmond of S.C.
32 Boo attachment
33 __ time (pronto)
34 Practical
35 Name for the Masters
39 __ and center
40 Encircled
41 Toronto's prov.
42 __ Arden
43 Wight is one
44 Puget and Pamlico: Abbr.
45 Some Old World snipes

47 Villa d'__
50 Four-time Masters winner
55 Eliminate gradually
58 Star: Comb. form
59 Dodge City marshal
60 Edge: Abbr.
61 Impassive
62 Some gifts
63 Host or giant follower
64 Mails

DOWN

1 Anti-infection agents
2 __ plaisir
3 Stares
4 __-trump (bridge bid)
5 Raucous
6 A neighbor of Minn.
7 Aspen is one
8 Riotous
9 Artificially high voice
10 Iron, e.g.
11 Actor Harrison
12 "Great __," 1929 song
13 J.F.K.'s successor
18 Chase
20 Carmine Beauty
23 Brazilian river
24 Legendary French hero
25 Small fish

26 Variety of beetle
27 Brook
28 "You never had it __!"
30 Ringside ringers
33 "__ a doctor in the house?"
36 Opens
37 Felt bad
38 Encroach
43 "Little we see in Nature that __": Wordsworth

46 Dwarf
48 Sample
49 Singer John
51 Features of elec. storms
52 Pinochle term
53 Goddess of discord
54 Angler's pole
55 Pod dweller
56 Actor Holbrook
57 Equip

ACROSS

1 Beluga's cousin
5 Hood who wasn't bad
10 Use radar
14 A tide
15 Dancer Fred's sister
16 Mah-jongg piece
17 M.V.P. at Ebbets Field
19 Within: Prefix
20 Coming out
21 Tattled
23 A son of Zeus
24 Andean country
25 Florida's Saint __ Canal
28 Corn unit
30 Household spirits
33 Antonym for fallen
35 Theater award
37 Actress Le Gallienne
38 Minute arachnid
39 Use a ladder for love's sake
41 Fast-talking
42 Suffix for court or front
43 Heraldic fur
44 Moon craft
46 Like Coleridge's mariner
48 Adjunct to 44 Across
50 Ridicule
51 Bellini opera
53 Preowned

55 Sloth
57 Ship's timber fastener
61 Algid
62 Hit song in 1919
64 River at Rennes
65 Red as __
66 Hindu offshoot
67 Gogol's "__ Souls"
68 Paris transit
69 Rigil Kentaurus, e.g.

DOWN

1 Story starter
2 Paper quantity
3 Stained-glass joiner
4 Assess
5 Hindu queen
6 Fyn Island seaport
7 Mintaka, Alnilam and Alnitak, e.g.
8 Kind of wind
9 Under, to Keats
10 Dallas of filmdom
11 Subject of "La Cenerentola"
12 Actor Ray
13 Vegas light
18 Concur
22 Unctuous
24 Riding whip
25 Vampire
26 An archangel
27 Summer-theater circuit
29 Expiate

31 Pandora unleashed them
32 Brinker footwear
34 Society-page word
36 A.F.T. rival
40 Tra __
41 Virtue
43 Sprite
45 Dress carefully
47 Caught a wink
49 T.S. Eliot's "__ in the Cathedral"

52 Palindromic title
54 Defunct alliance
55 Like some rain
56 Nat or Natalie
57 Waste allowance
58 Dismounted
59 Author-actress Chase
60 "Cowardly Lion" actor
63 Fortas or Ribicoff

ACROSS

1. An N.C.O.
4. Heathrow lander
7. Roadside boscage
12. Bourse
13. Nobleman
14. Mudflat
15. Agent: Suffix
16. Home of the Hawks
17. Hoopster Bird
18. Don Juan
20. Mound builders
21. Outraged
22. Like aviaries
24. Letters on a chasuble
26. Jubilant one
28. Indigo
29. ". . . thy warfare __": Scott
30. Obscurity
32. Voice
36. Was profligate
37. Fiendish
39. Ship-shaped table utensil
40. Sun god
41. Odds against this are 649,739 to 1
47. .001 of an inch
48. Novelist Aubrey
49. Pic
50. Cop a __
52. Jam-packed

54. Common contraction
55. Cannes lady friend
56. Sen. and H.R.
57. Soprano Lehmann
58. Deviate
59. Out of the wind
60. First lady in Parliament
61. U.S.N. grad
62. Kin of sts.

DOWN

1. Literary genre
2. Worldwide
3. Cylindrical
4. Ph.D. course
5. Trumpet call at the Globe
6. Sees if a suit suits
7. Spread out
8. __ Bator, Mongolia
9. Disciplinarian
10. Hardy cattle breed
11. Isle
12. Of an ancient Frank
13. Olla
19. Having a new life
23. Bricklayer's tool
25. Klondike vehicle
27. Withdraw, in a way
28. Contented sighs

31 Express vaguely
32 One of the Smiths
33 Part timers of a sort
34 Humphrey Clinker's creator
35 A long, long time
38 Like part of a circle
39 Hyde Park denizens

42 Freeholders of yore
43 East Indian sailor
44 Vast
45 Prospects
46 Shilly-shally
48 Agrippina, to Nero
51 Within: Prefix
53 Neighbor of Aus.
54 __ king

ACROSS

1 Long, feathery scarfs
5 Opposite the middle of a ship's side
10 Farewell, to Fabius
14 Italian currency
15 Mea __ (my fault)
16 Author Ludwig
17 Creamy cocktails
19 Bakery buy
20 High-backed wooden bench
21 Low, light carriage
23 Cornered
24 Sheriff's action
25 Basketball shot
28 Warp-knitted fabric
32 Word with cake or meal
35 __ Alamos
36 French school
37 S.C. university
40 Auction events
42 Songwriters' org.
43 Droop
44 Little one
45 Son in an Arnold poem
47 Ire
50 Key
52 Bowling-alley button
56 Aromatic herb

59 Engaged man
60 Instigate
61 Daisy or frosted cookie
63 Ticonderoga is one
64 Furthermore: Lat.
65 Dutch cheese
66 Greek cheese
67 Column part
68 Crandall and Ennis of baseball

DOWN

1 Explosion
2 Tex. athlete
3 Mountain ridge
4 Double trio
5 Anagram for cane
6 Kind of mite or moth
7 Cricket teams
8 "The cruellest month"
9 U.S.N.A. goat
10 Matador's move
11 Dart thrower
12 Caron role: 1953
13 A Fitzgerald
18 Alan from N.Y.C.
22 Flags
26 Middle Eastern org.
27 Free electron
29 Indianapolis athlete
30 Spread not fit for a bed

31 Assay
32 Edible tubers
33 Too
34 Cal or Georgia
38 Ohio city on the Ohio
39 Burst of energy
40 Dashed
41 Nog ingredient
43 Lecherous
46 Censures

48 Part of HOMES
49 Erected
51 Muse for Pindar
53 Slyly disparaging
54 Outer, to an M.D.
55 Pours
56 Rabble
57 Reed instrument
58 Spanish muralist
59 Chafe
62 Sal of songdom

ACROSS

1 Invoice
5 Mme. Bovary
9 Separate
14 An Adams
15 Biblical kingdom
16 The South
17 Ripped
18 Coffee servers
19 Utter
20 Fill with joy
22 American poet
24 Marie Wilson role
26 Comfort
27 __ Holroyd, "Bell, Book and Candle" witch
30 Knights' horses
33 United
34 Small sailboat
35 Crowded together
37 " 'Tis not __, or eye, we beauty call": Pope
39 Spicy savant?
40 Lower
44 Extinct ratite
47 Burnsian refusal
48 ". . . upon __ of Earth": Gray
49 Pitcher's place
51 Toulouse-Lautrec's birthplace
52 Pierce
53 China city

57 It's found inside banks
61 Triple Crown horse: 1935
62 Burden
64 John preceder
65 A wandering dog?
66 Sorghum
67 Place to come back to?
68 Opposites of thinkers?
69 Garden spot
70 Second Gospel

DOWN

1 __ noire
2 Lion
3 Italian coin
4 Soup ingredient
5 Feathered six-footer
6 Biting
7 "The __ Love"
8 Trouble for a tooth
9 Role Baruch played at D.C.
10 Cather subject
11 Imaginary Earth line
12 Puerto __
13 High-schooler
21 Author Ambler
23 Shakespeare's shrew
25 Barnyard bleat
27 Spur on

36

| | 28 | Bay | | 45 | Its cap. is Toronto |

28 Bay
29 Actress Vivien
31 Actress Keaton
32 American sculptor George
36 Feat
38 Roe who had a fishy pitch
41 Attentive
42 Pats
43 Embodiment
44 Govern badly

45 Its cap. is Toronto
46 At a great distance
50 In the same place: Lat.
53 Cross follower
54 That Melville novel
55 Rant's partner
56 Author Bagnold
58 Actress Miles
59 Asian ruler
60 Skating site
63 Abraham, to Terah

ACROSS

1 Hops oven
5 Place
10 Tonsure site
14 Camembert cousin
15 Silly
16 Andy's buddy
17 Company for rabid canines
19 Liquidates, in a way
20 Tokyo tender
21 Comedian Wilson
22 Portage burden
23 Place for 17 Across
26 Venerates
29 "Celeste Aïda," e.g.
30 Middle
31 Less irrational
33 Catered a banquet
36 What poor Uncle Harry wanted
40 "__ longa . . . "
41 Past or imperfect
42 Ely's river
43 Statesman Douglas-Home
44 Brought into balance
46 Gertrude Lawrence hit
51 Germanic inscriptions
52 Part of F.D.R.
53 Gowiddie, e.g.
56 Redolence
57 Costar of 46 Across and star of this puzzle
60 Outlet
61 Sired
62 King of the Huns
63 Contents of lodes
64 Manpower, afloat
65 Subject for a best seller

DOWN

1 Comply
2 "Judith" composer
3 Manifestation
4 __ quel (such as it is, in Tours)
5 Fine knits
6 "To think __ that's far away": Burns
7 College precincts
8 French article
9 J.F.K.: 1953–61
10 Tropical fruit
11 "The way to __ heart . . ."
12 "Happy birthday __"
13 Steel city
18 ". . . __ shall gain the whole world . . . "
22 The City of Victory
23 Banyan or baobab
24 "__ Macabre"
25 Vier predecessor
26 Minutes

27	Portal		45	Turndown
28	Spheres		46	Utah city
31	Because		47	Less refined
32	Burro		48	Golfer's hole-__
33	Mythical man-beast		49	Sovereign
34	Padraig's tongue		50	A type of mother
35	Gave hue		53	Jacques of film
37	Mercator work		54	A Gardner
38	Proper		55	Colliery entrance
39	Negative answers		57	A TV network
43	Turns away		58	Across, in poesy
44	Turns out		59	Bankroll

ACROSS

1 Demesne house
6 Purfle
9 Coll. houses
14 Run off to wed
15 Japanese woman diver
16 Lumberjacks' contest
17 Hock and sack
18 A buoy
19 In any way
20 Magpie's activity
22 Walled up
24 "__ Death": Grieg
25 First son
26 Thirty, in Paris
29 Veto
33 Some are controlled
34 Bank client
35 Wood sorrel
36 Causes of harm
37 Ordinance
38 Excels
41 Holey utensil
43 Makes believe
44 Welty's "The __ Heart"
45 Sister in a Chekhov play
46 Cablegram
47 Sale-seeking person
50 Key West, for Truman
54 Trace
55 Exile Amin
57 Leghorn's land
58 Predella topper
59 Cashew, e.g.
60 Radon, formerly
61 Burgess creatures
62 Episcopy
63 Canadian peninsula

DOWN

1 British royal stables
2 Lodged
3 Reprimand to tots
4 Producing an effect
5 Emulates Sam Adams
6 Suspends
7 Big bird
8 Salon treatments
9 Artist's activity
10 Round building
11 Opposite of apterous
12 Kind of vision
13 Auctioneer's cry
21 Lorna Ridd, __ Doone
23 Rialtos
26 March along
27 What some experiences do
28 Akin on mother's side

29 Vocal qualities
30 Gave the glad eye
31 Braid
32 Less used
34 Small, sweet oranges
36 Spree
39 Temporary
40 Aides
41 Job for some clerks
42 Sluggishness
44 Pandowdy
46 Emulate Rice or Oates
47 Type of party
48 Hawaiian city
49 Aware of
51 Has vittles
52 Askew
53 Actress Daly
56 Fitting

ACROSS

1 Hot seasoning
6 Stupid, clumsy fellows
10 Long-running TV hit
14 Navigational system
15 Bridge thrill
16 French magazine
17 Not together
18 Location
19 Barge
20 Routine
21 Conflicts
23 Bonnie Franklin TV hit
28 Fluffy fare
29 Actors' club
32 Viper
35 Torment
36 Radial, e.g.
37 MacLaine-Mitchum film: 1962
42 Argentine timber tree
43 Israeli airline
44 N.F.L. six-pointers
45 Bring together
47 Garbo and Nissen
49 John Ritter TV hit
54 Edmonton's province
56 Widow of Ernie K.
57 Sullen

58 Encourage
61 City in Fla.
62 Farm measure
63 College V.I.P.
64 Monetary penalties
65 Temper
66 Selvage
67 Lucullan event

DOWN

1 Mild cigar
2 Dr. Seuss's "__ Pop"
3 Heated
4 Violinist Jaime __
5 Savings acct. entry
6 C.I.A. forerunner
7 Boxing great
8 Rich political contributor
9 Small, silvery fish
10 Chow-hall friend
11 Les Whitten novel, with "The"
12 Type of gin
13 Chops
22 Suffer
24 Early pulpit
25 Once around Sol
26 Lodged
27 Animal chains
30 Thin wire nail
31 Emulates Dorcas
32 Aleutian island

33 Grown cygnet
34 U.S.S.R. bigwigs, once
38 Begot
39 Energy source: Abbr.
40 Japanese statesman
41 Babylonian neighbor
46 Goof
47 Harnessed
48 Coin
50 Paganini offering
51 City in Turkey
52 McKinley's birthplace in Ohio
53 Leavening
54 Rock star Ant
55 Crazy
59 Boffo producer
60 Chemical suffix
61 Switch position

ACROSS

1 Interstices
5 Guffaw
9 Neil Simon creation
13 Beginning of a Porgy song
14 Script direction
15 Any or some follower
16 Dippy or dotty
17 Acarid
18 Minor Prophet
19 Feature for Bismarck?
21 Feature for the Oz woodsman?
22 Rickles
23 Hole-__
25 A Titan
28 Mall component
29 Ukr., once: Abbr.
32 Dens
33 Hardy girl
34 Article
35 Feature for a Romeo?
37 Feature for a rebel?
40 A First Lady's monogram
41 Old English coins
43 Lascivious
44 Kind of curve
45 Plaintiffs
46 Have __ for news
47 __ noir (wine)
48 Apocrypha book: Abbr.
49 Feature for a wooden soldier?
52 Feature for an egghead?
57 Parting word
58 Mussolini's nickname
59 Adjutant
60 Relative of a toon
61 Cupid, to Plato
62 Ready and fluent
63 Chemical endings
64 Cousin of aren't
65 Pts. of time

DOWN

1 Oscar movie: 1958
2 Japanese isinglass
3 Kind of stick
4 Roman legion eagle, e.g.
5 Surround
6 W.W. II foe
7 Babylonian's rival
8 Supped
9 Ring up
10 __-majesté
11 Sector
12 Kind of book
15 Pule
20 Moat
21 Part of a statue
24 Has snacks
25 Rockweeds

44

26 Andersen output
27 Fact falsifiers
28 Sound system
29 Girl in a pool
30 Roe sources
31 Change the color of
36 Like a teenager
38 Disreputable person
39 Carryalls
42 President and king
45 Former French title of respect

47 Excuses
48 Throw out
49 Step
50 Utopia
51 Author of "The Immoralist"
53 Item to revere
54 Get one's goat
55 Of a Pindar work
56 Snares
58 Rep. of Indonesia before 1949

ACROSS

1 A way up
7 Pardoned
13 Large basket
15 Tableland
16 Elevate
17 Part of E.S.T.
18 Balanchine ballet
19 Burglars, e.g.
21 Jar cover
22 Campanella or Rogers
23 Serge-suit foe
24 Eat in style
25 Appear
27 Optical item
28 Scope
29 Shipyard area
31 "And thereby __ a tale"
32 Evict
33 Painful feeling
34 Calcutta cash
36 Early Mexican Indians
39 Send back
40 Sir Thomas, the writer
41 Roasted: Fr.
43 Place of exile: 1814–15
44 Esth, for one
45 Nylons mishap
46 Needlefish
47 Groups of lions
49 Steiger and Stewart
50 Language of Leonardo
52 Convention V.I.P.
54 Denies
55 Neptune's spear
56 Skillful ones
57 Puts forth effort

DOWN

1 Asparagus shoots
2 Danced in Argentine style
3 Pest
4 Not excluded
5 Tease
6 Ego
7 Bias
8 Freebie
9 Envelope abbr.
10 In a spin
11 Sailors' short ropes
12 Firth of Tay port
14 Choose the incumbent
15 Unskilled laborers
20 Connection
24 Peril
26 Nearsightedness
27 Mislay

28 Throw a tantrum
30 Piano music for four hands
31 Golfer Irwin
33 Omen
34 Akin
35 Offense
36 Took effect
37 Inquest official
38 Romberg's "The __ Prince"
39 Mezzo-soprano Resnik
40 Conduits
42 Map sections
44 Hillsides, to Burns
47 The Great Commoner
48 Angry
49 Sally of space fame
51 Once around
53 Tom of old westerns

ACROSS

1 Agree
5 Arctic Circle native
9 "Saturday Night Fever" music
14 Viva voce
15 Ancient Italian town
16 Arkin to Falk, in a 1979 movie
17 Big bundle
18 Negatives
19 Armadillo armor
20 Tactfully dismisses from a post
23 Even-steven
24 Sweet wine
25 Small spars
28 Windowed, in a way
32 Animated
33 Nimbus
34 Down Under bird
35 Dismisses
39 Chemical suffix
40 New Testament book
41 Plains abode
42 Abridgments
45 Stages
46 Apiarist's assets
47 Reduce a sail
48 Is dismissed, pirate style
53 Forearm bones
54 Aerial bombs
55 Cattail
57 Correct the camber
58 Opposed
59 Oscar's girlfriend?
60 Distributes
61 Actor Errol: 1881–1951
62 Funambulist's need

DOWN

1 Employer's offering
2 Saudi Arabian neighbor: Var.
3 Indonesian island
4 Optional
5 Eyepieces
6 Not sotto voce
7 Nest sound
8 Travelers' papers
9 Win over by persuasion
10 Egg on
11 Disparage
12 Mega-musical
13 Be indebted
21 Birds of prey
22 Pentateuch
25 Wise ones
26 Roman naturalist
27 Split apart

48

28 Compositions for two
29 Harvests
30 Roast host
31 Boxer's fists: Slang
33 Atavistic
36 Saharan sights
37 Merman or Waters
38 Mariner
43 Legally bind

44 Chinese ducks
45 Stomach enzyme
47 Right-hand page
48 Cloth ridge
49 Comstock entrance
50 Sharpen
51 Mysterious submarine captain
52 Jack of the G.O.P.
53 N.F.L.'er
56 Stain

ACROSS

1 Abbrs. on a plat.
4 One of the Cyclades
9 Capp's __ Slobovia
14 Cortés's quest
15 Toward a ship's left side
16 County in Mont.
17 Its only direction is S
19 Aunt in "Oklahoma!"
20 Naldi of the silents
21 Roman romances
23 Walk in space, for short
24 Descendant of Judah
25 An Arthurian damsel
26 Latin I word
27 Frog-to-be
29 Pilwiz
31 Sputnik launcher
33 Transuded
34 Pongo and Lar
37 Shooting match, in Sedan
39 Homophone for use
40 Shot
41 Porgy's woman
43 Finally
45 Dance center of a sort
50 Bakery implement
51 Jiggly salad

54 He helped raise folks to higher levels
55 Initials on a letterhead
56 Dusky
57 Maid of the __, at Niagara Falls
58 Related on the mother's side
60 Indian structure
62 N.B.A. pros Archibald and Thurmond
63 Name for a Hobby
64 Sun. talk
65 Assays
66 Vikings
67 Sharp road curve

DOWN

1 Wordsworth product
2 Russian transportation
3 Classified
4 Cry of disgust
5 Horrifies
6 Most spacious
7 Synthetic fiber
8 Cubic meter
9 Shoshoneans
10 Ward heeler
11 Dispute aggressively
12 Ennobles
13 Evaluated again
18 Diamond rain gear, for short
22 Diminutive endings

50

26 Lined up
28 Gets rid of
30 Suckling's forte
32 Eve, once
34 Insects' feelers
35 They use "gas warfare"
36 Of an age
38 One who pays
40 Wise
42 Scented bags
44 Playing marble

46 Coronation ostentation
47 Indolent
48 Certain threads
49 Chemical compounds
52 Quashed
53 Site of B.Y.U.
56 Mtg.
59 Holiday in Hanoi
61 "Maggie __," Beatles number

ACROSS

1 Shakespearean villain
5 Killer whales
9 Popeye's archenemy
14 Wait in concealment
15 Part of a bird's beak
16 Rajahs' wives
17 Dickensian embezzler
19 Pen name of novelist de la Ramée
20 Day of the wk.
21 Some are electric
22 He holds the bag
23 Ski lift
25 Hebrew letter
27 Untamed
28 Favorites
29 Wanes
33 Japanese aborigines
34 Set __ (make an appointment)
36 Movie studio
37 TV scoundrel
39 Ben-Hur's betrayer
41 "__ longa, vita brevis"
42 Civil-rights org.
44 Tries out
45 Sow chow
47 Actresses Claire and Balin
48 Pol. party members
49 __ of thousands

51 Hasten
52 Jewish law
55 Actor __ Everett
57 Old French coin
60 Close, to Cowper
61 Sam Spade antagonist
63 Flat
64 Slave
65 Burt Reynolds film
66 Dickensian murderer
67 Quarry
68 James Bond adversary

DOWN

1 Priam's grandfather
2 Atmosphere
3 Pluck
4 Trappist cheese
5 Shade of yellow
6 Virginia __
7 Peaked
8 Fall mo.
9 Coop group
10 "Annie __"
11 One
12 Time's fellow traveler
13 Glacial ridges
18 Gives way to an approaching train
22 Cheap jewelry
24 Use a bubble pipe
26 F.D.R. collection

26

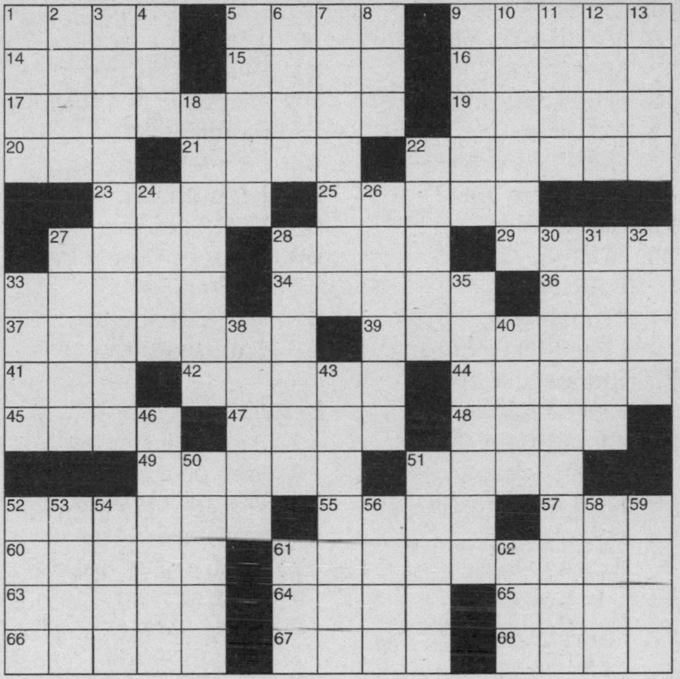

27 Gaelic cry of grief
28 Heathens
30 One who reviles
31 Lengths of cloth
32 Deps.
33 In __ (on the spot)
35 Actor Erik from N.Y.C.
38 Aquatic nymph
40 Bishoprics
43 Berra was one
46 Mexican food
50 Preserves
51 Wacky
52 Scottish goblet
53 Against
54 Boating problem
56 Present
58 Sonny portrayer in "The Godfather"
59 "Do __ others . . . "
61 Cooking abbr.
62 Minister's deg.

ACROSS

1 "Kidnapped" auth.
4 Greek letters
8 Musical-staff sign
13 Marksman's forte
14 Blood conduit
16 Bellowing
17 Does this drive gardeners loco?
19 Lasso loop
20 Arid plateau of S Africa
21 "Tobacco is a __. I like it.": Hemminger
23 Indian unit of weight
25 "I'm __ Baby," 1920's song
26 Paul and Phyllis
29 Loblolly
30 Eris's twin
31 Use a shuttle
33 Scottish and Irish tongues
37 Pandowdy
38 Food for swine?
41 Farrow from L.A.
42 Jewish feast
44 Antediluvian
45 Kind of burner
46 Spike a drink
49 Sang in Tyrol
51 Wheels for a samovar
54 "__ Flanders"
55 Nastily-treated politico?
57 Shy away from Elsie?
60 Italian painter: 17th century
61 Would this put a gardener in a fowl mood?
63 Derived from oil
64 High-strung
65 Unit of energy
66 "Games People Play" author
67 "L' __ c'est moi"
68 Faulty: Prefix

DOWN

1 Pool-hall frame
2 Pisa pocket money
3 Would this elude a gardener?
4 Disk-jockey bribe
5 Scatter seed
6 Made sore
7 Mug for suds
8 Made a gorge in
9 General __, former A.L. pitcher
10 He outranks a top kick
11 Soothes
12 A Flintstone
15 __ in the bucket
18 Climbs sharply in a plane
22 Tuberculosis drug
24 Contrary one
26 Babies' needs

27 An Iroquoian
28 Droop
32 Brace
34 "Bleak House" character
35 Emerald Isle
36 Hourglass filling
38 It makes perfect
39 Cambridge neighbor
40 Ancient land
43 Feature of stretchable fibers

45 Under
47 Crow's sound
48 Raise high rises
50 Agenda
51 Mont. county
52 Organic compound
53 High-pitched laugh
55 Splotch
56 Force or effort
58 Like Gothic yarns
59 Mtn. chains
62 Union foe: Abbr.

ACROSS

1 Radar sight
5 Duchess of __, Goya's friend
9 Lopez theme song
13 Wee-hour sound from the alley
14 Secure a ship
15 Greek dialect
16 Met highlight
17 Barrett or Jaffe
18 "For __ is the kingdom . . ."
19 First line of a rhyme
22 Lobster trick, e.g.
23 Half of MIV
24 Second line of rhyme
31 Punches for practice
34 Extraordinary fellows
35 Bee follower
36 Like some petticoats
37 Scholars' collars
38 River in NW Spain
39 Benchley's "Of __ Things"
40 Robe for Agrippina
41 Grind one's teeth
42 Third line of rhyme
45 Corrida cheer
46 Ladd and Alda
49 Last line of rhyme
55 Carroll girl
56 Town in NE Spain
57 Stagehand with a valise?
59 Consumer advocate
60 Take it easy
61 Faith follower
62 Rarae __
63 Drag strip for Ben-Hur
64 Ivan or Peter

DOWN

1 "Not __ long shot!"
2 Clown-faced sloth
3 "__ You Love," Humperdinck hit
4 Literary theft
5 Ambrosial drink
6 "Crazy" bird
7 Sound from Big Ben
8 "I smell __"
9 "Fuzzy-wuzzy had __"
10 Fetid
11 Queue
12 Top pitchers
15 Moral principles
20 Switch positions
21 Common scents
25 From head __
26 __ Gay, famous plane

56

27 French legislature
28 U.S.C. rival
29 Fish dish
30 Wife of Jacob
31 Do in
32 __ Alto, Calif.
33 Civil-rights org.
37 Memorable
Merman
38 Ignorant
40 Vendor
41 Big gap

43 Articulates
44 Trade
47 Fiddler and
pianist
48 __ cog (err)
49 Pet in "Peter Pan"
50 King of Norway
51 Wait patiently
52 Arias
53 Motorist's "downer"
54 Seep
58 __ capita

ACROSS

1 A neighbor of Sicily
6 Slang word for 9 Down
9 Below par
13 Not natural
14 Lahore wrap
15 Nagy of Hungary
16 Actor Arnold
17 Like a teardrop
18 Thersitical fellows
19 Oater heavy
21 Patella area
22 Trotsky or Uris
23 Domain
25 Whence Cervantes wrote "Don Quixote"
29 Relic
31 "There'll be __ time . . ."
32 Singer Clapton
34 Con game
37 Corpus __
39 Puts in Newgate
42 Per
43 Expanse
45 Although, to Antony
46 Olympics site: 1988
48 Holdings
50 Corrupt
53 Fine wood
55 Err
56 Second-story jobs
62 Cell, e.g.
63 Venezuelan copper center
64 Sculptor's product
65 Snorri story
66 Like Manute Bol
67 Addax's big cousin
68 Hammer, in a way
69 Spanish articles
70 Lacoste and Clair

DOWN

1 Mixture for cattle
2 Countertenor
3 Fabulist
4 Basis of decimal system
5 Shakespearean deputy
6 Early designer of flying machines
7 Dies __
8 Emulate Raffles
9 The Artful Dodger, e.g.
10 Saudi Arabian's neighbor
11 Fiat
12 View anew
14 London district
20 Article of faith
24 File sect.
25 Walk; tramp
26 Syngman of 46 Across

58

27 Kansas town
28 Cop's quarry
30 Calif. campus
33 Move up
35 Nora's terrier
36 Is obliged to
38 Ice-cream flavor: Abbr.
40 "Love Story" star
41 Pandowdy
44 Walks a beat
47 Sale's offer
49 Debi Thomas is one
50 __ throat
51 Diminish gradually
52 Vacuum tube
54 On a par: Fr.
57 Russia's __ Mountains
58 Function
59 Mashhad site
60 Medieval domestic
61 Does lawn repair

ACROSS

1 Long N.F.L. pass
5 Roman earth goddess
10 Crazy
13 Asseverate
14 Young ox
15 Challenge
16 Appellation
17 Stage
18 Fitzgerald or Raines
19 Ponder with pleasure
21 Start of a quote by Aristotle
23 Thunder god
25 Tra-__
26 Quote: Part II
30 Crown
34 Teachers' org.
35 Tidy
36 This once went far
37 Carp or flounder
39 Joseph in Egypt
41 Poses
42 All
44 Streamlet
46 Life story, for short
47 Della from Detroit
48 Quote: Part III
50 Freshwater duck
52 Liberal side
53 End of quote
57 "The __ Sanction": Trevanian
61 Stravinsky or Gorin
62 Concerning
64 Hub
65 Homophone for sleigh
66 British money
67 Singer Campbell
68 Countdown starter
69 Put at bay
70 Play area

DOWN

1 Loud noise
2 Ellipsoidal
3 Note
4 Respiration
5 Cookbook abbr.
6 Heavenly
7 Study
8 Outcome
9 Betel-nut palm
10 African country
11 Woody's boy
12 Cathedral official
15 Particulars
20 At that time
22 A chorister
24 Of ample girth
26 Construe
27 Pont Neuf waterway
28 Sample
29 Kay or Ringo
31 Excuse in a whodunit

32 Relative magnitude
33 Heated crime
36 Ferret
38 Forte of S.E. Morison
40 Extremely rough action
43 Rod's adjunct
45 "__ With Father"
48 Shop tool
49 Like Scrooge

51 Adjust
53 Stallone movie
54 Eye amorously
55 Sorrel's cousin
56 Hackman or Wilder
58 Fete
59 At all
60 Tear
63 Kennedy or Williams

ACROSS

1 Once, once
5 To-let items, in want ads
10 Search thoroughly
14 Wild hog
15 Acclaim
16 Cap-__ (entirely)
17 Adriatic wind
18 Card game (variety of seven-up)
19 Torn
20 Jack Nicholson vehicle: 1970
23 Verve
24 Author of "The Tell-Tale Heart"
25 Between mars and mai
27 Coming twice a year
32 Discharge
33 Throb
34 Architect I.M.
35 Dumas trio
39 Cape
40 Early Olympics site
41 "__ vincit amor"
42 Recondite
45 Old Greek measure of length
46 Wall St. term
47 British servicewoman
48 O. Henry 1906 publication

55 Fifty percent
56 Male lead in "Carousel": 1945
57 Like two peas in __
59 Succulent plant
60 "__ Mood," 1939 song
61 Darnel
62 Not any
63 Quoted
64 Poll-taker Roper

DOWN

1 Recede
2 Housetop
3 Hindu garment
4 Cross over
5 Abrogation
6 Indian, for one
7 Early auto manufacturer
8 Astor or Pickford
9 Block
10 Lurch from side to side
11 Oil-cartel acronym
12 "__ eyes have seen . . ."
13 Wagers
21 The finest
22 Charged atom
25 Turkish officials
26 Left-hand page
27 Fundamental
28 Writing fluids

29 Defeat
30 High perch
31 Actress Eilbacher
32 Peut-__ (perhaps): Fr.
33 Hungarian dog
36 Kind of oxide
37 The whole thing
38 Make feeble
43 Chewy candy
44 D.D.E.'s domain in W.W. II

45 Like some nuts
47 Flexible twig
48 Holier __ thou
49 Nimbus
50 N.C. college
51 Hindu queen
52 Berra's gear
53 Iridescent stone
54 A Crosby
58 __ volente (God willing)

ACROSS

1 Doctors' org.
4 Turkish city, formerly Seyhan
9 "__ of Fools," 1965 film
13 Leslie Caron film: 1953
15 Did a cobbler's job
16 Deli order
17 Charlton Heston movie: 1967
20 Wins over
21 Hatred
22 Call __ day
23 Map abbr.
24 Al Pacino movie: 1975
33 A first name in mysteries
34 Gossage or Goslin
35 Town in New Guinea
36 Rossellini classic: 1946
38 Balaam's __
39 Crème de la crème
41 Wartime agcy.
42 Reach by radio
44 Full of reverence
45 Tatum O'Neal movie: 1976
49 Mouths
50 __ excellence
51 He played in "A Thousand Clowns": 1965
54 Baby's perch, in a rhyme

58 Rock Hudson movie: 1968
61 High flier at sea
62 Lustrous
63 In the near future
64 Peruse
65 Hammer and sickle
66 Salamander

DOWN

1 Grossglockner is one
2 Temperate
3 Jai __
4 Off the right path
5 Condemn
6 Landon and a sitcom
7 Seine
8 Sticks
9 Flower part
10 Indian from Ariz.
11 "__ a Kick Out of You"
12 Nosegay
14 Concave aspects of curves
18 "I could __ horse!"
19 Beef Wellington, for one
24 Military warehouse
25 Plant of the goosefoot family
26 Move effortlessly
27 "You __," Klugman sitcom
28 He choreographed "Pippin"

29 ". . . and a time __":
Eccl. 3:7
30 A part of Gdansk
31 Horse opera
32 Necessities
37 Biblical mount
40 Ophelia's brother
43 Unyielding
46 Gave orders
47 Pays out
48 Folk singer–political
activist

51 German quaff
52 "God's Little __":
E. Caldwell
53 Russian
river
54 Josip Broz
55 Stir up
56 Chinese horn
57 Univ. teacher
59 Niño's uncle
60 Formicary
inhabitant

ACROSS

1 Lens aperture
5 Fodder plants
10 Jettison
14 She's back in town
15 Seaport in SW Japan
16 To __ (exactly)
17 Gen. Patton
20 Command to a horse
21 Helm position
22 Showy bird
23 Weaving defect
24 Climbs up
26 Alfred E. Smith
30 One of the Greats
31 The Tent Maker
32 Retrieving dog, for short
35 Rip apart
36 Sudden energetic spurt
38 "Cavalleria" temptress
39 Pilcorn, e.g.
40 Hardens
41 Type of type: Abbr.
42 Ehrich Weiss
46 Inculcate
49 As well
50 "My __ days,/When I was green . . . ": Shak.
51 Wave on la mer
52 Alias, for short
55 Perry of the Bears
59 Czech name for the Elbe
60 Pleasant changes
61 Asian desert
62 Compass points
63 Motionless
64 Mimed

DOWN

1 Move with difficulty
2 Marsh bulrush
3 Word with shoppe
4 Place for darts
5 "__ they build . . . ": Young
6 One-celled animal
7 Uncivil
8 Letter from Piraeus
9 Honorific Japanese suffix
10 Printer's obelisk
11 Driver's maneuver
12 Apportioned
13 Mosquitoes, e.g.
18 Covered with Alençon
19 Restaurateur's concern
23 Hastened
24 What Venus de Milo is missing
25 Thailand, once
26 Edible submarine
27 Tract
28 Four noggins
29 Cook without liquid

32 Louis Marie Julien Viaud	**45** Addict	
33 Lyricist __ Jay Lerner	**46** Basket fiber	
34 Romantic island	**47** U.S. naval historian	
36 Espied	**48** Freshman cadet	
37 Plan for building lots	**51** Seine feeder	
38 Beach resort	**52** On the peak	
40 Teacher's decision	**53** Japanese seaport	
42 Stares angrily	**54** Saharan	
43 Closet adjunct	**56** Faith, in France	
44 Adjective for Methuselah	**57** Sought elective office	
	58 Moslem chief	

ACROSS

1 Ice-cream flavor
6 Box
10 Injury
14 "Oklahoma!" aunt
15 Deli offering
16 State or river
17 Frighten
18 Spoken
19 N.Z. parrots
20 Weak
22 Ingests
23 Lincoln Ctr. attraction
24 Welcome time for employees
26 Motley crowd
30 Walk heavily
32 Exhausted
33 Targets for some kickers
37 Suggestive look
38 "Thoughtful" flower
39 Boat's central structure
40 Daily dozen
42 Room in a Greek temple
43 Mehitabel's companion
44 Ambush
45 Sealskin boot
48 Misspeak
49 Hillside dugout
50 Helplessly; inevitably

57 Leonine sound
58 Certain savings accts.
59 A.k.a.
60 Den
61 Moslem judge
62 "Beau __": Wren book
63 Indian meal
64 Patella's location
65 Organic compound

DOWN

1 Denote
2 Earthenware pot
3 Symbol of silence
4 Basil, e.g.
5 A West Point graduate
6 Young hog
7 Beautician's specialty, for short
8 Native of Oman
9 Rotund
10 Chicanery
11 In the van
12 Lariat
13 Like some tree trunks
21 Reade's "__ Woffington"
25 Elec. unit
26 Respiratory sound
27 "Family Ties" member
28 Merriment

68

29 Note of a robin or lark
30 Rabbit
31 Girl
33 Cut
34 Vend
35 Anatomical tissue
36 Destroy
38 Dickens character
41 French vineyard
42 Slaughter
44 Twisted
45 TV actress Gibbs
46 W.W. I menace
47 Poisonous snake
48 Miss Dinsmore
51 Asian country
52 Take on cargo
53 Small land masses in the Seine
54 Itemize
55 Recent
56 French river

ACROSS

1 Zeus' sister and spouse
5 Scraps
9 Woody fiber
13 Claude's chapeau
14 Glimmer
15 German industrial region
16 Manna from heaven?
18 Siouan
19 Intrepid
20 Evil spirits
22 100 centesimi
23 Forthwith
24 Thrills
27 El __ (rich spot)
28 Beholden letters
29 Film critic, e.g.
31 Supple
34 Campus service org.
36 Hogtied
38 Plant shoot
39 Frome of fiction
41 "__ Grows in Brooklyn"
43 Examine carefully
44 Nymphs on Mt. Ida
46 Spuds
48 Little pistils
50 Kind of car or phone
51 Engross
52 Esoteric

56 Physicist Niels
57 Why he left grad school?
59 Redact
60 A dollar is one
61 Noted conductor
62 D.C. group
63 __ peur (fearless)
64 Central point

DOWN

1 Goddess of youth
2 A son of Aphrodite
3 Insurrection
4 Studio for Seurat
5 Flora and fauna
6 Zoological suffix
7 Threefold: Comb. form
8 "__ but wiser"
9 Trite
10 Why they eyed the showroom?
11 Glistened
12 Chignon part
13 Estop
17 College treasurer
21 Abbr. after a list of names
23 Boll weevil, e.g.
24 Ireland, to Gaels
25 Swag
26 The Caine or the Pequod?
27 Agr., etc.
30 Natterjacks

	1	2	3	4		5	6	7	8		9	10	11	12
13						14					15			
16					17						18			
19								20	21					
			22				23							
24	25	26				27								
28				29		30			31				32	33
34			35		36			37		38				
39				40		41				42		43		
		44			45			46		47				
48	49						50							
51					52						53	54	55	
56				57	58					61				
59				60						61				
62				63						64				

32 Gardener, at times

33 Tolkien creatures

35 Some house adjuncts

37 Abhor

40 __-do-well

42 Loesslike

45 Saint __, city in Vt.

47 Manolo Ortega, e.g.

48 Tree trunk in a Scottish sport

49 Dwelling

50 Whose Rose?

52 Mil. command

53 Employed

54 The home team, e.g.

55 Suffix with Siam

58 Profane, in Pahoa

ACROSS

1 Subsides
5 City on the Aar
9 Goat's offspring
12 Ivy League school
13 Fattened rooster
14 Hardy's "__ the Obscure"
15 Essayist
16 Carrot's cousin
17 Author Gardner
18 First word of an Isaac Goldberg quote
20 Door sign
21 "Henry VI" character
22 Jug's kin
23 Quote: Part II
31 Farm structures
32 Menacing March day
33 Magician's item
34 Takes to court
35 Called by loudspeaker
37 Corn dish
38 Chemical suffix
39 Luxurious
40 Subordinate
41 Quote: Part III
45 Hill dweller
46 Abate
47 Lax
50 Quote: Part III

55 Actor Douglas
56 Beat
57 Atop
58 TV award
59 Leans
60 A lunchtime
61 End of quote
62 Confederate
63 Descry

DOWN

1 Ogled
2 Indonesian island
3 Radar set image
4 Eared pinnipeds
5 Tropical fruit
6 Noyes's "Drake," e.g.
7 Blushing
8 Compass dir.
9 Author Vonnegut
10 Still
11 Forest animal
13 Carved gem
14 Swedish soprano Lind
19 They're played in Reno
20 Time periods
22 Like some cars
23 "A Doll's House" playwright
24 Spa feature
25 Kilmer poem

26 "The __ of the Iguana": Williams
27 Presidential initials
28 Whiplash
29 Asian city
30 Forever, in poesy
35 Byron, e.g.
36 Donkey's uncle
37 Forest dropper
39 Panther color?
40 Skirt style
42 Not neat or stylish

43 Jackson bill
44 Clock parts
47 Twist
48 Tall-growing bean
49 Troops
50 Labor
51 Ship's frame
52 A son of Seth
53 "Bus __," Inge play
54 Actor Curtis
56 School org.

ACROSS

1 Celebration of the Eucharist
5 Low, marshy land
10 Works with needle and thread
14 Domestic feudal slave
15 Buenos __
16 Askew
17 Work of the Founding Fathers
20 Hurricane center
21 Plunges briefly
22 __ Domingo
23 N.J. five
24 Like some wheels or keels
26 Speculative plan
29 Mortgages
30 Roof overhang
31 Mass of glacial ice
32 __ Branco, Brazil
35 What 17 Across sets forth
39 Feminine suffix
40 An Oliver
41 Opposed
42 Asimov product
43 Clergyman Mather
45 To the nth degree
48 Rizzuto, e.g.
49 St.-Cyr-l' __, French town
50 Virginia of Va.
51 Windmill sail

54 Chief U.S. law officer
58 Sharp
59 Sea eagles
60 Year in Claudius I's reign
61 Orch. section
62 Henbit and yarrow
63 Netman Wilander

DOWN

1 Allot
2 Pallid
3 Koko's weapon
4 Wall St. watchdog
5 Soundness of reason
6 Small amounts of smoke
7 __ and sciences
8 Oahu garland
9 Vt. clock setting
10 Fiends
11 Patrick of the Knicks
12 Inscribed
13 Assembly of churchmen
18 Central European river
19 Income from wealth
23 Christmas
24 Estuary
25 A daughter of Laban
26 Ornamented wig
27 Cries of surprise
28 Twain's "__ Diary"

74

29 Southpaw
31 Wretched
32 Rave's partner
33 Division word
34 Valhalla deity
36 Deer horn
37 What the ewe grew
38 Recent
42 Formal drawing rooms
43 Fondle
44 __ sesame

45 East Indian trees
46 Group of eight
47 Burden carrier
48 Imprisoned
50 Unit of force
51 A Met score
52 "Hurry up and __"
53 Yalies
55 Unused
56 Previous to, in poesy
57 Shade tree

ACROSS

1 Moslem spirit
6 British spirit
11 Horned god
14 "The Tempest" spirit
15 Julian's jars
16 Ellington's monogram
17 Noisy spirit
19 Inlet
20 Recent: Prefix
21 Spume; froth
22 Fighting spirit, colloquially
23 P.O. abbr.
25 Utah's flower
27 Mischievous spirit
30 Memorable pianist
33 Jewish folklore spirit
37 Faultily made
40 __ air painting
41 A victim of Artemis
42 Attention
43 Actress Hasso
44 Word with firma or cotta
45 Reject
47 Dumbarton Oaks, e.g.
49 Graf __
50 Small boy
51 Muffins
53 U.S. mil. honor
55 Spirits
58 Maxim
61 Scotch explorer
64 René's spirit
65 Irish spirits
68 Resort
69 The heavens
70 Heart parts
71 Successor to F.D.R.
72 To eat, in Bonn
73 Army of the Potomac leader

DOWN

1 As. nation
2 Golf club
3 Pale green
4 Colonist's Indian friend
5 __ du Diable
6 Old Genoese bigwig
7 Olive genus
8 Ecstasy
9 Thrashed
10 Still
11 Persian spirit
12 Actor Tamiroff
13 Tide status
18 Golf cup
22 Grotesque spirit
24 Vocalize
26 Roms
27 Ham it up
28 Spirits in Pompey's pad

76

29 She toys with boys
31 Pochard
32 Some pinnipeds
34 Sired
35 Utah range name
36 Fastened, in a way
38 Search for food
39 Faucet problem
46 French spirits
48 Family of an Irish patriot
52 Jrs.-to-be

54 Wickerwork hamper
55 Lave
56 Mischievous spirits
57 Adroit
59 Dryad's home
60 Sea swallow
62 Invisible emanation
63 Partner of Geraint
65 Sheltered side
66 Part of a western
67 Thus, in Glasgow

ACROSS

1 With 68 Across, subject of this puzzle
7 Film coscenarized by 68 Across: 1954
14 Less sane
16 Radial sellers
17 Anthony of fiction
18 Salty Asian expanse
19 Norman's woe?
20 Hostler's milieu
22 Corporeal channel: Comb. form
23 Sacred
25 Kind of card
27 Pasch
30 Microwave oven no-no
34 With 40 Down and 67 Across, phrase created by our subject
37 Larch's kin
38 Shell adjunct
39 Owned
40 Evian, e.g.
41 Tackle
42 What fools do
44 Eskimos, Utes et al.
46 Gary product
47 Showers icily
48 21st Amendment
50 Musette pipe
54 Ancient Asian
57 Sp. province and city
60 Roof finial
61 Flatter, in a way
63 Vitamin C sources
65 House occupant
66 Chandelier, e.g.
67 See 34 Across
68 See 1 Across

DOWN

1 Israeli port
2 Where to see chaps
3 "Portnoy's Complaint," e.g.
4 Map dir.
5 Letter opener
6 Assay
7 Less fresh
8 Broadcast
9 "Breast-work"
10 One with a yarn
11 "__ Tired," Beatles song
12 Poetic adverb
13 Premed subject
15 Did a knee jerk
21 Pitcher Saberhagen
24 Type of man
26 Tell
28 For a short time
29 Actor Penn
31 Rotate
32 Etcher's need
33 Chairman's supporters

34	Rocky peaks	51	Moslem princess, in India
35	__ monde (high society)	52	"Otello" is one
36	Ancient tongue	53	Iron, in Essen
37	Graf follower	54	SE China's __ Bay
40	See 34 Across	55	Aussie bird
43	Galileo, to Pope Urban VIII	56	Studio spinner
44	Jai __	58	Seed covering
45	Kind of bar or pod	59	Former German state, to Frenchmen
47	Cuts	62	Summer quaff
49	Parisian pies	64	Degree preceder

ACROSS

1 Decline in value
4 Howled
9 A solid
13 Frenzied
15 Call forth
16 Author Whitely
17 In general
19 Italian commune
20 Character on a typewriter
21 Former V.I.P.'s in Istanbul
23 "__ We Got Fun?"
24 Income for a Lourdes landlord
25 Worn away
28 Joins
31 Kyoto coin
32 Rooms: Sp.
34 Actor Leon
35 Some mos.
37 __-law (a relative)
39 Vital fluids
40 Calif. border lake
42 Shades
44 Lincoln's "Cap'n __"
45 Attend the World Series, e.g.
47 Become conscious
49 Military bigwigs
50 Three, to Hans
51 Chair parts
53 Systematic article
57 Roosted
58 TV documentary: 1976–82
60 Wild Wilder
61 Rock projections
62 Limping
63 Twelve __, "G.W.T.W." plantation
64 Limestone region
65 John __ Passos

DOWN

1 Island in the West Indies
2 Alcott and Carter
3 U.S.N.A. mascot
4 Pope heroine et al.
5 Cease! at sea
6 City on the Ouse
7 Hosp. procedure
8 Become more profound
9 Good gift for a hostess
10 In hot water
11 Vamp of the silents
12 Students at New Haven
14 Work dough
18 Becomes sere
22 Biographer Edwards
24 Item for Menuhin
25 Islets
26 Tire or summary
27 Out of order
28 Prau, e.g.

29 __ Annunziata, Italian resort
30 Liquidated
33 Family of a 20's–30's tennis star
36 Xenophon's teacher
38 Trouble spot
41 Coup d'__
43 Assert as true
46 __ as a dog
48 Gee chaser

50 Bottom of the barrel
51 Granulated starch
52 Words from Belli
53 Peter or Paul
54 "If __ a thousand sons . . .": Shak.
55 Vaughn role in ". . . U.N.C.L.E."
56 Salamanders
59 F.D.R.'s Blue Eagle

ACROSS

1 Dog's bane
6 Zola heroine
10 B.&O. stops
14 Reluctant
15 Confrere of Yves and Calvin
16 Inventor Elias
17 Bewildered
18 A '66 role for Burt
20 Palpitatingly
22 "Pretty little poppy" of song
23 An intermission follower
25 Amphora
28 South African iris
29 Greek letter
33 Id __
34 Revise
35 Beg
36 Uncompromising
38 __-Magnon man
40 Giraffe relative
41 Rice dish
42 Support a seditionary
44 Citizen of Vientiane
45 Wind: Comb. form
46 Pedicel
47 Hemstitches
48 Transaction
51 Sentimental twaddle
54 Dancer Duncan
58 Retaliation
60 __ Abdel Nasser
61 Ernie K.'s widow
62 Huckleberry
63 Encampment
64 Wands
65 Boswell or Burns
66 Thickheaded

DOWN

1 Set-to
2 French novelist: 1850–1923
3 National League division
4 Parade command
5 Condition
6 Harmless
7 Maple-seed wing
8 The Silver State
9 Old World lizard
10 Party chatter, sometimes
11 A W.W. II prime minister
12 M.P.'s concern
13 ". . . __ fine picture": Goethe
19 A big win
21 Vitriolic
24 Fertilizer
25 Wasp genus

26 "Addams Family" member John
27 Monument of a sort
30 Famed portraitist
31 Oblong fruit
32 Farewell, in Cancún
34 Implement a law
37 Storms
39 Tractable
43 Outback birds

46 Lovely to look at
47 Calm
49 Norwegian kings
50 Blustered
51 Kalinin, formerly
52 Modernize, perhaps
53 Site of Phillips U.
55 Mideast land
56 Knocks
57 Out of the wind
59 U.S.N. top dog

ACROSS

1 Tasman discovery: 1643
5 Teutonic god of thunder
10 Actress Witherspoon
14 Shebat's follower
15 Lyric poem
16 Foreboding
17 Ridicule
18 "West Side Story" heroine
19 Rave's cousin
20 Wapiti
21 Wimbledon champ: 1983–84
23 Sheepshank, e.g.
25 Mao __-tung
26 Leatherneck
28 Namesakes of Isolde's lover
33 Some tests
34 Desert
35 Soak timber
36 Greek commune
37 "__ Went to Haiti," 1939 song
38 Betel
39 Wind dir.
40 Had sauerbraten
41 Shucks!
42 Portuguese export
44 Praise
45 Joplin opus
46 Bakery worker
47 Wimbledon champ: 1937–38
53 Pertinent
56 Like a bump on __
57 Synthetic fabric
58 Yachting
59 Skid-row denizen
60 Devilfish
61 Fake
62 Anon
63 Writer Mme. de __
64 A Dumas

DOWN

1 Réclame
2 Admired one
3 Wimbledon champ: 1947
4 Annoy
5 Lower in grade
6 Bright fish
7 Urth or Skuld
8 Take __ view
9 Nuclear adjective
10 Zinke
11 Gen. Bradley
12 Vegas rival
13 Bellum preceder
21 Vickers and Voight
22 Being, in philosophy
24 Aswan's river
26 Fashions
27 Denver's McNichols __
28 Places for chapeaux

84

29 Mosby specialty
30 Wimbledon champ: 1975
31 Thread: Comb. form
32 Vt. ski center
34 Kegler's area
37 Realms
38 __ Royale, Mich.
40 TV adjunct
41 A gait
43 St. George's foe

44 Army's __ Corps
47 Grackles
48 Salmagundi
49 "__, Nanette"
50 Dennis the Menace
51 Cubitus
52 Love to excess
54 Seckel, e.g.
55 Tractable
58 Cerastes

ACROSS

1 Moslem prayer leader
5 Upright
10 Capella, e.g.
14 Actress Maris
15 "The Wreck of the Mary __," 1959 film
16 Leander's love
17 Pretentious official
19 Saarinen
20 One, in Dundee
21 Bounder
22 Typewriter part
24 Bounded
26 Weird
29 Chemical suffix
30 Ike's opponent
31 Cheerleader's word
32 Cooper's __ Bumppo
34 Mauna __
36 Early auto
38 Disarrange
39 Menorah, e.g.
42 Japanese parliament
44 "The Greatest"
45 Moray
46 Like some seals
48 Pasture
50 Luigi's fish
54 Rickenbacker, for one
55 Long
57 Frome of fiction
58 Paso __, Calif.

60 Indian port
62 Santa __, El Salvador
63 Beige
64 Looking-glass Land denizen
68 Short, erect tail
69 "Les Troyens," e.g.
70 Interdiction
71 Subdue
72 Violet-family member
73 German river

DOWN

1 African antelope
2 Lamented
3 Toughen
4 D.D.E. in 1920
5 Author Ferber
6 More rubicund
7 Cochlea site
8 Grand __ (wine-bottle words)
9 Conductors' concerns
10 Mets' home
11 Small top
12 Checks
13 Andy and Mickey
18 Gambler's delight
23 Deighton or Dawson
25 Taste
27 More ancient
28 Ostrich's kin

33 Charm
35 Political org.
37 Brit. honor
39 Thinking goes on here
40 A memorable Grasso
41 Abrogate
42 "Mommie __": C. Crawford
43 A bestseller in 1984
47 Congo red, e.g.

49 City on the Maine
51 Like arbors
52 King of England: 1017–35
53 Captivate
56 Bar, in law
59 Paving tool
61 An Anita of songdom
65 New Deal agcy.
66 Poetic contraction
67 Second name

ACROSS

1 Welty's "__ Wedding"
6 Not very bright
9 Floor, in Paris
14 French girlfriends
15 Opposite of WNW
16 Grease jobs, for short
17 The Big Apple, originally
20 Serves
21 Stroll
22 Past or future
24 Nothing
25 Commotion
26 Scrap
30 Collection of Norse poems
34 Ring name
35 Onset
36 Primp
37 Big name in 17 Across
40 Conceits
41 Greek name for Greece
42 Be situated
43 Mandrels
44 Locust and loquat
45 North Sea feeder
46 Prefix for angle or pod
48 Declares
50 Contradict
52 Rival of Captain Absolute
54 Records from Hudson to Giuliani
59 Catkin
60 Airport abbr.
61 Hogan's cousin
62 What some people storm
63 Pile
64 Conform

DOWN

1 Pop
2 Flightless bird
3 Sozzled
4 Craft: Comb. form
5 Residues
6 Profound
7 Adherents
8 Choo Choo Coleman was one
9 Varnish ingredient
10 Glasses
11 First shepherd
12 Hereditary unit
13 Sum, es, __
18 Rains icy particles
19 Hugo work
22 "Holy" city
23 Corrected copy
25 An ungulate
27 Assessor
28 As __ (usually)
29 Mode
31 Casino employee

32 Gainsays
33 Sweetens the pot
35 Grads-to-be
36 Foot, to Fabius
38 Town near Huntington, W.Va.
39 Italian artist: 16th century
44 Row upon row
45 Tried
47 Disorders

49 Goddess of the hearth
50 Synagogue platform
51 Pitcher
52 Movie dog
53 Fellow
54 Arrest
55 Knowledge
56 __-Locka, Fla.
57 Tie fabric
58 Thus far

ACROSS

1 Germinated grain
5 Kefauver
10 Atlanta arena
14 To __ (exactly)
15 Pathetic
16 Garish light
17 Musial's nickname
19 Fix a leak
20 Parasol
21 Viva voce
23 Alpenstock's cousin
24 Mature
25 Pyromaniac's crime
28 Rain check of a sort
30 Suave
33 Used a Baedeker
35 World Series M.V.P.: 1975
37 Between phi and psi
38 Actress Velez
39 Finished a nap
41 Hide
42 Goddess of infatuation
43 Hydroplane
44 Francis of films
46 Suit fabric
48 Algonquian from Wis.
50 Peripheral
51 Pancake
53 " . . . a bug in __"
55 Pallas __
57 Rx person
61 Tab
62 Branch Rickey's nickname
64 Harold of old comics
65 Finished 18, with "out"
66 Chess piece
67 Chesterfield
68 Backbone
69 Venetian V.I.P.

DOWN

1 Congeries
2 Aleutian island
3 Like Miniver Cheevy
4 Two hundred
5 Patriot Allen
6 Rated, at Flushing Meadow
7 Domesticated
8 Stat for Clemens
9 Vatican event
10 In the bullpen
11 Carl Hubbell nickname
12 N.F.L. coach Chuck
13 Very dark
18 Title for Macduff
22 Trojan horse, e.g.
24 Murderous frenzy
25 Paper size
26 U.S. 1 is one
27 Allie Reynolds's nickname
29 Fragrance
31 Ridge or crest
32 Pirates' slugger: 1946–53
34 East Indian transport
36 One of seven

1	2	3	4		5	6	7	8	9		10	11	12	13
14					15						16			
17				18							19			
20									21	22				
			23					24						
25	26	27				28	29			30			31	32
33				34		35		36				37		
38				39	40						41			
42			43					44	45					
46		47			48		49		50					
	51			52			53	54						
55	56			57						58	59	60		
61			62	63										
64			65					66						
67			68					69						

40 Sage
41 Lazy one
43 Gossip-column word
45 Place for a niblick
47 New Orleans neighbor
49 Bizet opera
52 Primrose and bridle
54 Skier's maneuver

55 New Testament book
56 Dr. Huxtable's son
57 Where heros are made
58 "And __ . . . have not been idle": Russell
59 Inversion problem
60 Casino portion
63 Flight on a shuttle

ACROSS

1 Mexican sandwich
5 Dog's bane
9 Escape
14 Payment for Charon
15 Mislaid
16 Venerable, to Virgil
17 Scram
20 Changed
21 Ab __ (from the beginning)
22 Canadian export
23 American thrush
24 Title for Emma Bovary
25 Ballet bird
26 Feminine suffix
27 Balletic knee bend
29 Actress Woodard
30 Patron saint of cripples
32 Obscures
33 Deeply
36 Hawed's partner
37 Dissolute dandies
38 Photographer Diane
39 Stop up
40 Target of Philip Wylie
43 "South Pacific" ingenue
44 Campanella or Rogers
45 Bakery bonus
47 Orch. section
48 Court follower
49 Ebbs
51 Scram
54 S-shaped moldings
55 Famous sister ship
56 "Fish Magic" painter
57 TV actress Volz
58 Ben Adhem
59 Fast fliers

DOWN

1 Start of a Hemingway title
2 White poplars
3 "The Dam Busters" composer
4 More antiquated
5 Drifting sea ice
6 Mountbatten, for one
7 Superlative finish
8 Awaiting visitors
9 Alpine sound
10 Chou En-__
11 Illicit
12 Blockheads
13 Ancient group of mystics
18 Use a spider
19 Night before
24 Penurious
25 Wild plums

27 Walk wearily
28 O.T. book
29 Sheltered, at sea
30 Entire range
31 March 15, e.g.
32 Puff
33 Birthright
34 Started out
35 Kanga's baby
36 U.S. fashion
   designer
39 Type of cigar

40 Paragons
41 Egg concoction
42 The common people
44 Automaker's
   monogram
45 "__ Du Lieber . . ."
46 Exudes fumes
48 TV's "__ Living"
49 Gambler's town
50 A son of Isaac
52 Ending for auction
53 Projecting end

ACROSS

1 Square column
5 Weaving defects
10 Spoil
13 Former Spanish coin
14 ". . . neither cast ye your __ before swine": Matt.
15 Shoshonean
16 Holiday desserts
18 Havana Mrs.
19 Members of a fourth-century sect
20 White House nickname
21 Suffix with axiom
22 "La __ Vita"
23 Dessert filling
25 Gas: Comb. form
27 Not so bold
28 Pierre's soul
31 Pt. of Q&A
33 Varnish ingredient
36 Thanksgiving tradition
41 Zodiacal sign
42 French vineyard
43 Initials at Pensacola
44 Helping theorem
47 Prime for a crime
50 Thanksgiving sauce
53 Quoted
57 Mental vagueness
58 Roman's 2001

59 Biological hollow
60 G.I. address
61 Thanksgiving main course
63 Err
64 __-camp (military secretary)
65 Vishnu incarnation
66 Asner and Begley
67 Bamboo, e.g.
68 Hebrew letter

DOWN

1 Hungarian hero
2 Nerve: Comb. form
3 Native of Sri Lanka
4 Guanaco cousin
5 A mem. of Congress
6 Bay of Naples island
7 __ Hound (Canis Major)
8 Whiten
9 Draft org.
10 Enlists as a private
11 Entrance courts
12 Respond to a stimulus
14 Greek letters
17 Leg joint
21 Eastern bigwig
23 Chinese dynasty
24 Gaelic country
26 Skate, e.g.
28 Workers' gp.
29 Avril follower

94

30	Celebrates; proclaims	48	Beige
32	Pouch	49	__ del Fuego
34	One __ million	50	Pursue
35	"Thumbs down" letters	51	Fast
37	A Castle	52	Loses a lap
38	Elia	54	Hungarian wine
39	Waiter's need	55	See 33 Across
40	Center of activity	56	Israeli general
45	Biographical item	59	Ingested
46	Fleet	61	Tatter
		62	Thanksgiving scores: Abbr.

ACROSS

1 Goals
5 Twiggy broom
10 One of a cautionary trio
14 Boodle
15 Soprano Lucine
16 Malay canoe
17 Incredible
19 Layers
20 Hemoglobin deficiency
21 Table doily
23 Pops' partners
25 Gawk
26 London and Paris, e.g.
30 Heretofore, to the Bard
33 Brings home the bacon
34 Egyptian dancing girls
36 Heredity transmitter
37 Long, exhausting march
38 So long, in Sevilla
39 Mint
40 Knight or Weems
41 Speedy
42 Béarnaise, e.g.
43 Critter
45 Cold-shouldered
47 Round dance

49 __-majesté
50 Wry expressions
53 Gamuts
57 Amplitude
58 Incredible
60 Polynesian demon
61 Natterjacks
62 Mine entrance
63 Nickname for Elizabeth I
64 A Lauder
65 Cincinnati team

DOWN

1 Famed lioness
2 This may be proper
3 Inside info
4 Skier's maneuver
5 Type of grass
6 Second-largest bird
7 Coarsely ground corn
8 Certain exams
9 Dugongs' cousins
10 Area
11 Incredible
12 Chaplin's widow
13 Ancient history
18 Donnybrooks
22 Favorite U.S. transporters
24 "Susie" author: 1947
26 Pelota basket
27 German city

1	2	3	4		5	6	7	8	9		10	11	12	13
14					15						16			
17				18							19			
20							21			22				
			23		24		25							
26	27	28					29		30				31	32
33					34		35					36		
37				38							39			
40			41						42				
43			44				45		46				
		47				48		49					
50	51					52		53			54	55	56
57				58			59						
60				61						62			
63				64						65			

28 Incredible
29 Wilier
31 In the bag
32 Declined
35 Motorist's day's-end quest
38 Earmark
39 List or register
41 Part song
42 Lazy __
44 See 23 Across

46 Read carefully
48 Cuban dollars
50 Kind of bag
51 Mechanical procedure
52 Rodin output: Abbr.
54 He wrote "Isabelle"
55 Novelist Bagnold
56 Corps.' bosses
59 Epicedium

ACROSS

1 Smears
6 Tut's home
10 Mosque minister
14 Shoelace tip
15 20th-cen. calamity
16 Dayukku, for one
17 Matthau-Jackson film
19 Jewish month
20 Hudson River city
21 German dramatist-critic: 1729–81
23 Action onstage during an ovation
26 Hunt's partner
27 Miler Sebastian
28 Word denoting excess
29 Ostrich's look-alike
31 Small monkey
33 Gov. or Sen.
34 Receive a benediction
36 Infamous collar item
38 The cold shoulder
42 Pedestal part
43 Breathing passage
44 Do gardening
45 __ contendere
47 Nautical notes
48 Willing
49 Blue
51 Guitar's kin
53 Was impassioned
55 Capital of Me.
57 Theme-dominated times
58 Perfumery input
59 Streisand-O'Neal film
64 Rialto light
65 A Hebrides island
66 Early American patriot
67 Termination points
68 Triangular structure
69 QB John

DOWN

1 Lah-di-__
2 Of yore
3 Eskimo's curved knife
4 Move
5 Area to the rear
6 P.G.A. champ: 1986
7 Temple athlete
8 __-feuille (type of pastry)
9 Halve
10 "__ corny as . . ."
11 City in SE Alberta
12 Hersey town
13 On-ramp sign
18 Convincing, polemically
22 Circles around
23 Conks
24 Elliptical
25 Fine!
26 Inane

30 Giants' successors
32 Conway or Holt
34 Hummocks
35 Jay of comedy
37 Fanciful being
39 Tokyo, formerly
40 Boring tools
41 Emulated 6 Down, with "up"
46 Think faster
48 Evangel

49 River to the Rhone
50 "The Ascent of F6" co-author
52 Western resort
54 Bea Arthur role
56 Vases
57 Suzette's state
60 Actress Harding
61 Crow's cousin
62 Three __ match
63 Baseballer Ron

ACROSS

1. Chanteuse Edith
5. Ordained teacher
10. Prologue's antecedent
14. Aleutian isle
15. Great Lakes tribe
16. K-P connection
17. Broadway gas
18. Newspaper section
20. Very burdensome
22. Vent
23. Desire
24. Some railroad workers
26. Winchman
30. "_ gratia artis"
31. Trademark
32. Rave's partner
34. _ accompli
38. Church corner
39. Copenhagen or Marengo
41. _ no good
42. "One man's _ is another man's Persian"
43. Sped
44. Eight bells
45. Simple enzyme
47. Bobbin holder
49. Tack sellers
54. Opposite of clerical
55. Cactus opening
56. Stretch
61. Inflated currency
63. Flag
64. Joy's lioness
65. Jagged
66. Tear
67. Prophet
68. Challenged
69. Theater area

DOWN

1. Hunger spasm
2. Brain passage
3. Yours, in Lyon
4. Sense of humor
5. Some oil companies
6. Sussex river
7. Crosby namesakes
8. Artist Shahn
9. "This _ Life"
10. Okla. national park
11. Sufficient
12. Derisive look
13. Wrongs, to Darrow
19. Groan inducers
21. Society bud
25. Abhorrers
26. Quahog
27. Apple type
28. Ripened
29. Terrier or snitcher
33. Modernist
34. Musical about Fanny Brice

35 Footless
36 Chemical suffix
37 Franchot
40 Arranged, as troops
45 Friend in need
46 Appeared
48 John, in Aberdeen
49 Yeggs' targets
50 As __ (generally)
51 Obtuse

52 Germanic counterpart of Thor
53 __ Wences
57 __-majesté
58 Martian: Comb. form
59 Bell sound
60 Punta del __
62 Sixty minutes, in Siena

ACROSS

1 Chilling storyteller
4 Dryden's "__ savage"
9 Bar chaser
13 Qualified
15 City that grew tired
16 Pindar poems
17 Flowery greetings
18 Painter Dufy
19 What nuns take
20 Competitors for Edgars
23 "__! poor Yorick": Shak.
24 Sun god
25 Seven singers
28 When-and-where info
33 Cloverlike plant with yellow flowers
35 Man of La Mancha
36 Future fish
37 King's march site: 1965
39 Keresan Indian
40 Off-the-cuff words
43 State of caution
46 Cowboy stories
48 Vandyke's cousin
49 Australian pest
50 Eavesdroppers' plants
51 Love-story coterie
58 Branches
59 Gershwin's "Sometime Thing"
60 Zoological suffix
61 Grand Canyon St.
62 Pedro's friend
63 Marsh
64 Fountain of music
65 Early riser?
66 Hairy primate

DOWN

1 It may make dates
2 Petruchio's imperative?
3 Flash Gordon and Frank Merriwell, e.g.
4 Tells stories
5 Gives the go-ahead
6 Sweat producer
7 Frown: Var.
8 Uncle Sam's plea
9 Short tales
10 Skunk's protection
11 Report from Rather
12 Snaky shape
14 Possessions
21 Pre-H.S. grades
22 Pedal extremities
25 Kind of vote
26 Disappear gradually
27 Strips
28 Hamburger accompaniments
29 It's the top
30 Gore
31 Cacophony
32 Delete
34 Faculty bigwig

38 "Yet I __/Against Heav'n's hand . . .": Milton
41 List individually
42 Speaker's platform
44 Academic gown
45 Computerized stock figs.
47 Landing strip
50 Blows one's own horn
51 Uncommon
52 Leave out
53 Request to "ye faithful"
54 Suffix re blood condition
55 Neighbor of Col.
56 Harvest
57 Wise man
58 Shoot the breeze

ACROSS

1 Simon's dividers
5 Desert regions
9 Easy as __
12 English rock duo
13 Burin or dibble
14 "Aloha" synonym
16 Wool, in Madrid
17 Where to find Guantánamo Bay
18 Fervor
19 Drugstore cowboy's look
21 Something to punch
23 Comfort
25 Concoct or contrive
26 "A Life for the __"
27 Garden figure
28 Sarcle
31 Barbary Coast port
34 Delivers
36 Lifeline location
37 Toothy expression
38 Showed disdain
42 Vessel for Nelson
45 Monogram of a Duke
46 Author of "The College Widow"
47 Act like a vandal
48 Rocker __ Ant
49 Shenanigans
52 Cheaters of sorts
56 Asian nanny
57 Drive of note
58 Germany's industrial heart
60 Chemical compound
62 Whence pizzas come
63 Inkling
64 Divagate
65 End of a Sandburg title
66 Kind of paper
67 Appear

DOWN

1 Saddler's instrument
2 Pandemonium
3 Brando's Paris dance
4 Petty
5 The balance: Abbr.
6 Wood-working machines
7 Asian desert
8 The big house
9 Ray of filmdom
10 Union that doesn't charge dues
11 Irish county
14 Golfed grossly
15 Dashiell contemporary
20 Lessen
22 This has a soffit
24 Erskine or Maxwell
28 Juno her name?
29 Skip
30 Man "seen" in an anagram

31 Altar's alcove
32 Gangly
33 Kind of club
35 Kitchen helpers
39 Dashboard items
40 Red-coated dairy product
41 Black mark
42 Streaker's cousin
43 Darling or Howard
44 Whit

48 Egyptian deity
50 Mohawk transportation
51 Rough prodding
52 Homer's one-horse town
53 Operated a loom
54 Canzoni
55 Uncouth
59 Butter at Fordham
61 Moon-landing apparatus

ACROSS

1. Hood's weapon
5. Sea of __, in Russia
9. British naval base, __ Flow
14. Convex moldings
15. Joan Sutherland, e.g.
16. Rel. study
17. Having wings
18. Singles
19. Tars' tales
20. Comic's special delivery?
23. "Trinity" author
24. __ in wait (lurk)
25. Dialect
28. Hymn of praise
33. Suffix with cell
34. __ B'rith
35. Duos: Abbr.
36. Capital stationery?
40. Qt. or pt.
41. Portico for Pericles
42. Part of a meet
43. Foretell
46. Cubic meters
47. Sterlet delicacy
48. Quartet
49. Composition by Helen's abductor?
56. Cheerful
57. Comedian Sahl
58. __ off (calm down)
59. Carroll girl
60. Spice or weapon
61. Nobelist for Peace: 1984
62. Became dried up
63. The last word
64. Bachelor's party

DOWN

1. Uncertain effort
2. Entire: Comb. form
3. An attendant on Cleo
4. Heifetz and Iturbi
5. Object of Venus's affection
6. Chemical elements
7. Across the plate
8. Amphora
9. Golf term
10. Oratory
11. Air: Comb. form
12. Player on the dealer's right
13. Smith and Jolson
21. Mirador
22. TV sitcom "Kate and __"
25. Mountain lions
26. Cottonwood
27. Scout's rider
28. Irk
29. Pumice
30. Kind of berth

106

1	2	3	4		5	6	7	8		9	10	11	12	13

31 One of the Horae
32 Little helpers?
34 Greek letter
37 Resource
38 Ease
39 Emulates Cabotin
44 Stupor
45 Entertained
46 Mitigate
48 Higher power in "Star Wars"

49 Cumulus
50 Rabbit's burrow
51 Hall of Fame educator __ Willard
52 Gallivant
53 Rummage about
54 Minim
55 Relative of a snail
56 Ethiopian title

107

ACROSS

1 A variety of ruby spinel
6 Reject a suitor
10 Jacks of clubs
14 "One man may __ horse . . ."
15 Man from whom Edomites descended
16 Pastoral piece
17 "To be __ to be"
18 Bridle part
19 Poet Pound
20 Niggler
22 Building girder
23 "__ Rides Again," 1939 film
24 Genetic component: Abbr.
25 Saarinen
27 Careless, in Cannes
31 Grant and Natalie
34 Reduce via a fixed ratio
36 Time period
37 __-walsy
38 Unite
39 Hundred-pound boxer, e.g.
42 Alienates
44 Kind of income
45 Gyrate
47 __ Lanka
48 Asian wild sheep
52 A Marx
55 Out of fashion
58 Prefix with lateral
59 Golfer Wayne __
60 Error's partner
61 Bandleader Columbo
62 Actor Estrada
63 He worships: Sp.
64 Chaucer's Wife of __
65 Ye __ tea shoppe
66 Arcade or ante preceder

DOWN

1 Flaxen
2 Eagle's nest
3 Elongated fish
4 Took as one's own
5 Voltaire's forte
6 Nerd
7 Words of understanding
8 Abode for Simba
9 Wine cask
10 Mottled
11 Axlike tool
12 Vidal's "__ Breckinridge"
13 Bridge bid
21 Saint-__ (French West Point)
22 He wrote "A Loss of Roses"
24 Depend (on)
26 A Siouan
27 U.S. caricaturist's family
28 Hawkeye State
29 Actress-dancer Verdon

30 Some are tight
31 Something woven
32 Sweetheart of Alley Oop
33 Cameo stone
35 Baseball Hall of Famer's initials
37 Philippine tree
40 Bad-tempered
41 River in N Spain
42 Electronic bug
43 Fencing position
46 Cry of contempt

49 Suffix with commend
50 Acquire knowledge
51 Marquetry
52 Thyme, e.g.
53 Bluish green
54 Oxidize
55 European blackbird
56 Roman poet
57 Small child
59 Fifth sign of the zodiac

ACROSS

1 Soprano Frances __
5 Spanish home
9 Shocking
14 Enlist again, as a G.I.
15 Current units, for short
16 Nemo's creator
17 Relative of a via
18 Da's opposite in Moscow
19 Zones
20 Part of H.R.E.
22 Bitter vetch
24 Sniggler's catch
25 "Vive __"
26 French politician Daladier
28 Cantankerous
30 New Orleans cuisine
33 Kin of 5 Across
35 Some mass-media employees
36 Brewer's product
37 Thick
40 Cereal grass
41 Unit of magnetic induction
44 Flax holders
47 Oil-yielding seed
49 Emulates a peacock
50 Sinister
52 Thicket
55 Divan
57 Bench warmer
58 Former Dodger pitcher Claude __
59 A.F.B. near Valparaiso
61 Wend, e.g.
63 Towel word
64 Obliterate
65 Buster Brown's dog
66 Natural linen color
67 Tritons
68 Disfigurement
69 President of South Korea: 1948–60

DOWN

1 Rebel angel in "Paradise Lost"
2 "__ Go, Lover," 1954 song
3 Guarantee in the Fifth Amendment
4 Deductive
5 Bamboo stem
6 A Carter
7 Describing a trial guarantee in the Sixth Amendment
8 Houston athlete
9 Gardner of films
10 "Her lips __ . . .": Coleridge
11 Guarantee in the First Amendment
12 Single
13 Minus
21 Russian hemp
23 Juice, to Pierre
26 Wilhelm's ground
27 Macaw

29 Terminate
31 Page
32 Tolkien group
33 Things to tip
34 Word in a log
38 Letter opening
39 Siam or Sudan ending
42 Tibetan monk or nun
43 "__ Blue?": 1929 song

45 Gumshoes
46 Franken's "__ Language"
48 Print measures
51 Bounces
53 Talon, in Tours
54 Follow
55 Spotted
56 Scarebabe
58 Atop
60 Readings on vanes
62 Ottoman's V.I.P.

ACROSS

1. Deck unit
5. Without
9. O.T. book
13. Melville work
14. Stuff
15. "Symposium" author
16. Bunk
18. Spartan serf
19. Clever
20. Kit's partner
22. Bull
24. Days of yore, of yore
25. Alien in a sitcom
28. Minute
29. A beast of the chase
31. Skirmish
33. Outgrowth
36. Minn. neighbor
39. Ellipsoid
40. Hokum
41. French department
42. Worn-out horses
43. Designer Fogarty
44. Dance spot, for short
45. "__ Souls": Gogol
47. School subj.
49. Gee opposite
50. Fuss
52. Applesauce
56. Drumbeater
58. Characteristic auras

62. De Mille–Copland ballet
63. Horsefeathers
65. Estuary
66. Cannonballed
67. Cows, formerly
68. Emblem of Wales
69. Footless
70. Tons

DOWN

1. Stupor
2. __ Jacobs (Danny Thomas)
3. Type of canal
4. Bakeshop offering
5. Contrive
6. "Exodus" character
7. Cartoonist Bushmiller's strip
8. Vilify
9. Dairy-department item
10. Bosh
11. Maldives unit
12. Was weakminded
15. Snap
17. "The Minister's Wooing" writer
21. Billy carrier
23. Juicy fruit
25. __ patriae
26. Clothier Strauss
27. Baloney
30. Missile or tank starter

112

32 "What __ is new?"
34 Drama by Euripides
35 Reagan's Attorney General
37 Spanish chest
38 __-nothing (ignoramus)
40 Attacked
44 Frank product
46 In progress
48 Made the hair curly

50 Millay's "Second __"
51 Parasite
53 Greek coins
54 Flag
55 Canal sights
57 Far from aggressive
59 Drudgery
60 Rosacea
61 Slanting
64 King or Court status

ACROSS

1 Eject
5 "Awake and __!": Odets
9 Gets along
14 Chigoe
15 Pointed arch
16 Moslem law council
17 Mushroom-shaped
19 Himalayan country
20 Dockers' org.
21 Hudson or Maxwell
22 Avril follower
24 Cuckoo
25 Word in a Heller title
27 Secular
28 Forefront
29 Organic compound
30 Arab's outer garment
32 Matador's red cloth
34 Dallies
36 Puts on cargo
37 Evanescent
40 Medieval sons of the soil
43 Botanical beards
46 Sherman Act's targets
48 Bro, e.g.
49 Actress Lanchester
51 Ages upon ages
52 "__ my lady . . .": Romeo
54 __ out (deletes)

55 A hallucinogen
56 O.T. book
57 English river
59 Jockey's short whip
60 Actress Skala
62 Emit flashes
65 Obviate
66 Isaac's elder son
67 "Deutschland __ Alles"
68 Caterpillar's bristles
69 Descartes
70 Soviet news agency

DOWN

1 Part of O.P.A.
2 Wailing
3 Thesmothete
4 Word with end or line
5 Chesterfield, e.g.
6 Stravinsky
7 Saul's grandfather
8 Bud of a plant
9 Bundle of nerve fibers
10 Pub item
11 Did a road job
12 Arise
13 Calif. river
18 "__ bin ein Berliner": J.F.K.
23 Object
26 Dover sight
27 E. Indian sailors
30 Pain: Comb. form

31 Arthur or Lillie
33 Continued
35 Criticize severely
38 Eur. country
39 Midnight follower
40 Dallas and Stevens
41 Causing wear
42 Small barrel
44 "Arabian Nights" hero
45 Social and political classes

47 Sault __ Marie
50 Michaelmas daisies
53 Deduce
54 Australian bird
57 Family group
58 Chills and fever
61 Author Levin
63 "How __ doth breed a habit . . .": Shak.
64 Furrow

ACROSS

1 Maligns
8 Howlers in the wild
13 Grammatical error
14 In-and-outer on Wall Street
16 Start
17 Walked with determination
18 Finished
19 "__ of Me," 1931 song
21 Freight-hauling trailers
22 Victory signs
23 Perfume component
25 Greek commune
26 Sounds of hesitation
27 Reached a high point
29 Wallet item
30 Ingests
31 Plain
33 Roman magistrate
36 Puts forth effort
37 Piles up
39 Victim
40 Ribbed fabric
41 Accompanies
43 Chart
46 Poorly proportioned
48 Relief pitchers' goals
49 Visit
50 Instruments for Yo-Yo Ma
52 Sleep researcher's abbr.

53 Magna __
54 Drill sergeant's command
56 Pertaining to a river bank
58 Device for removing cherry pits
59 Mailer novel, with "The"
60 __ nous
61 Decrees

DOWN

1 Calif.'s __ Pass
2 Slurs
3 Celebrations
4 This turns litmus red
5 "__ Carlotta," T.A. Daly poem
6 Sights at Palm Springs
7 Extracts metal from ore
8 U.S.M.A. grads
9 Scraps
10 Revealed
11 Mileage gauge
12 Dregs
13 Strainer
15 Takes umbrage
20 Overdue
23 Ingenuous
24 Turns back
27 __ célébre
28 N.Y.'s First Family: 1873–75

30 Curve shape
32 An actress in "L.A. Law"
33 Bolivar's birthplace
34 Brunch item
35 Pastry article
38 Cicatrix
39 Head of a Canadian province
42 Expend too much effort

43 Contralto Anderson
44 Offering places
45 Part of a platform
47 Factory
49 Wrist bones
51 Elbe feeder
53 Dear, to Don Giovanni
55 Homophone for air
57 Natural soil aggregate

ACROSS

1 Lettuce type
5 Soap plant
10 Earp weapon
14 Celebes ox
15 Stuffed
16 Cosmetic ingredient
17 Mencken quote: Part I
20 Draft agcy.
21 Pan invented by Barrie
22 Redford is one
23 Farm equipment
24 Diminutive suffix
25 Happens
28 Handled a lacrosse ball
32 Roman way
33 Bounders
34 Stop __ dime
35 Quote: Part II
40 British ref. book
41 An Algonquian
42 Network of nerves
43 Squash
45 Scorpio's heart
48 Hairpiece
49 Germ cell
50 Capital of Jordan
53 Composer Erik
54 Warbuck's friend, with "The"
57 End of quote
60 One of three B's
61 Delusion's partner
62 Swill
63 Loom part
64 Unit
65 Yorkshire river

DOWN

1 Duo before "black sheep"
2 Khans
3 End products of snips, snails and certain tails
4 A word from Marley's partner
5 Too
6 Dull surfaces
7 "The __," Tryon novel
8 Lascivious look
9 Old English letter
10 Saw at poker
11 Airplane's __ strut
12 Cut of meat
13 Care for
18 Translucent silica
19 Khakass, for one
23 Avon resident
24 An official language of Pakistan
25 "With a little __ luck"
26 A Barrymore
27 "__ cold and starve a fever"
28 Fire
29 Born follower
30 Growing out
31 Oasis products

33 Young Fidel's pal
36 Navigation instrument
37 Chemical suffix replaced by ide
38 D.D.E. in W.W. II
39 Dies __
44 Like many tabloids
45 Wingless female aphid
46 Spread a rumor
47 Waste allowance

49 "Bonjour Tristesse" author
50 Clerical garb
51 Word after corn or oat
52 Medieval weapon
53 Chinese: Comb. form
54 Elba reversal
55 Kind of gin
56 __ up (invigorates)
58 Mil. decoration
59 Adherent

ACROSS

1 Holy Grail, e.g.
6 Crocks or shocks
10 Initial quartet
14 Mennonite
15 Declare openly
16 Lunar sea
17 Old Latin American coin
18 Whit
19 Draftee's status
20 Sydney swim stroke?
23 U.N. member, once
24 Small hole
25 Least
29 __ diem
30 Catchall abbr.
31 Bellow
34 That is, to Cato
39 Dangerous Donetsk gamble?
42 Treacherous person
43 Congressional creations
44 "Man of __," 1934 film classic
45 Lowell or Alcott
47 Zealous
49 Mistakes on paper
53 Profoundly wise
55 Manchurian marble game?
61 Polonius advised against this
62 Tamarack or tamarind

63 "Zoo Story" dramatist
64 Theater org.
65 Sicilian city
66 Jewish month
67 Kind of mate or work
68 "The Third Man" director
69 Niagara power-system designer

DOWN

1 A Vishnu incarnation
2 Ostrich's cousin
3 Toppers
4 "Lord, __ I?"
5 Kind of line
6 Incarcerates
7 Weight system, for short
8 Tournament agenda
9 S.C. Foster's river
10 Love, in Livorno
11 Devoid of originality
12 "Sara __," 1887 children's classic
13 Apportioned
21 Stars over the Forum
22 Actor Ritchard
25 First name in talk shows
26 Small case
27 Abrade
28 Additional

29 Locale for a figurehead
32 "Drink to me ___ . . ."
33 Altar on high
35 Kind of end or heat
36 To be, in Toulon
37 Jazzman Getz
38 Big top
40 Hot under the collar
41 Established practice
46 Piece or mind preceder
48 Fashion anew

49 Fanfare
50 Lyon's department
51 Cow catcher
52 Former Indochinese kingdom
53 ___ of the crime
54 In the lead
56 Marine raptor
57 "The Twittering Machine" painter
58 Declines
59 Authentic
60 ___ good example

ACROSS

1 Gold-rush name
7 Collectors' items
13 Contemplative
14 Having social success
16 Place for materiel
17 Herb for the cook
18 Party fare
19 Mighty hunter
21 Cicero's 104
22 Buck's mate
23 Scarf
24 __ in arms
25 Word with eclipse or module
27 Spruce
29 Roman road
30 Regard highly
32 Glad tidings
34 Some W.W. II fliers
36 Give off
37 Part of vitamin B complex
40 "She __ to Conquer": Goldsmith
44 Indian of Manitoba
45 Winglike
47 Corpus Christi native
48 Minus
49 Peninsular country
51 Biographer Winslow
52 Mornings: Abbr.
53 Large merchant ship

55 Abner's father
56 Carouse
58 Mineral from a Russian range
61 Silk fabric
62 Warms up again
63 Not encroaching, in football
64 Ancient Palestinian ascetic

DOWN

1 Earnest
2 Left over, as a shopper's money
3 Literary monogram
4 Word with ear or can
5 Dwight of the Red Sox
6 Living remnant
7 Playful
8 Matador's victim
9 Mimicked
10 Phiz
11 Pacify
12 Fla. island
13 Implement for Hiawatha
15 Red __, children's game
20 "Utopia" author
23 Source of betel nuts
24 Hallux
26 Houses on peaks

28 Pins
31 "I Remember __"
33 __-gritty
35 Ornamental open work
37 Vibrato
38 Revolutionary War mercenary
39 Euro-American defense gp.
41 Rival of a Cantabrigian

42 Atelier item
43 Traps
44 Bow or Barton
46 Obliteration
50 Trichords
53 Yours, in Tours
54 Foxx from St. Louis
57 Some sweater sizes: Abbr.
59 Sighs of contentment
60 Actress Remick

ACROSS

1 Corn mush
5 Sugar cube
9 Acoustic unit
14 Dwarf buffalo
15 Inter __
16 A planet
17 Invoice
18 Vidal book
19 Participated at Henley
20 Syrian city
22 Futile
24 Ovid's "__ Amatoria"
26 Vex
27 Land in a river
30 Foxier
34 S.A. nocturnal prowler
36 Roman Hera
37 Ariz. Indian group
38 Ivernian's land
39 Outer: Prefix
40 With 56 Across, first words of St. John's Gospel: Lat.
43 Wail
44 Catchall abbr.
45 "Thus __ Zarathustra"
46 Sins
47 Barn topper, sometimes
48 Michaelmas daisy
49 Retirees' agcy.
50 Last mo.
51 Droop
53 Orion neighbor
56 See 40 Across
61 Kind of alley or date
63 Instrument for Orpheus
65 Ligurian Sea feeder
66 Pier
67 Before long
68 Forms a lap
69 Stadium areas
70 Beatty film
71 Book after Joel

DOWN

1 One of the Leewards
2 Indigo plant
3 Infiltrating spy
4 Insect's sensor
5 Cabinet Department
6 Eskimo knife
7 Spanish artist Joan __
8 Potentially dangling verb forms
9 Ghost
10 Word from the woebegone
11 Red-tape expert
12 Adherent: Suffix
13 Cain's land
21 Zoroastrian
23 Khomeini's kin
25 Sensational
28 Exhaust's opposite
29 Bugler, for one

124

30 Stimulates the punch
31 Head and eye followers
32 Essential
33 Merits
35 Sect chaser
36 General purpose vehicles
41 In no way
42 Inedible orange
50 Dandies
52 Plant
54 Male ant
55 "Auld Lang __"
57 Tabula __ (clean slate)
58 Part of a cup
59 "Do __ others . . ."
60 Caribou's food
61 A sandwich, for short
62 Oahu garland
64 Scepter

ACROSS

1 Of the Vatican
6 Every sock has one
10 Toby, e.g.
13 Sky blue
14 French Revolution song
15 Chopper
16 "Lust for Life" star, Irish style
18 Over there
19 She raised Cain
20 Actress Andersson
21 Poe's lost maiden
23 Poet Thomas
24 Shak.'s era
25 Cod's cousin
28 Slangy dissent
30 N.J. five
33 Western, e.g.
36 Bedded down snugly
38 "Queen __," former TV show
40 Opening book division
41 Sends on, as a letter
43 Actress Luise
44 Novelist Seton
45 Nick and Nora's dog
47 Zounds!
48 __ Spee
50 Leaves out
53 The wherewithal
55 Well-heeled
56 U.S. space observatory
59 Sinatra's second
60 Final big battle, Irish style
63 Buddhist discipline
64 Adult insect
65 Milkmaid's milieu
66 Tolkien forest giant
67 Scruff
68 Building afterthought

DOWN

1 Walk the floor
2 Black Sea arm
3 Chaste
4 Noah's floating zoo
5 __ the nose (dominated)
6 France's W.W. II line
7 Feel poorly
8 Clanging vehicle, Irish style
9 Atelier item
10 China's Long March leader, Irish style
11 Caesar's wife
12 Dancer Kelly
14 Kind of heel
17 Troubled waters' soother
22 Gay __, gaslight decade
23 Du Pont's state
25 Missing union leader
26 O'Neill's "__ for the Misbegotten"

27 "Houseboat" star, Irish style
29 Seal's baby
31 __ barbae (barber's itch)
32 Bergen's Mortimer
34 Author LeShan
35 Solid ground, Irish style
37 Indian monkey
39 Football gains: Abbr.
42 Kind of battery
46 Friend, to Pablo
49 With full force
51 "__ am of Irlonde": Anon.
52 Pola's rival
53 Stun
54 Place for a roast
56 Chief god of the Aesir
57 Skirt insert
58 Cameo stone
61 Tourist's aid
62 Duryea or Dailey

ACROSS

1 Vulgarian
5 Footless
11 Krazy __
14 Melancholy
15 Mohammed's daughter
16 Uris hero
17 Porter on space travel
19 Command to Fido
20 Mucilaginous
21 "Anthem" author
22 Only's partner
23 Ga. neighbor
24 Porter on sauerbraten
26 Intimate group
29 Rational
30 G.I. address
31 An Adams
33 __ effort
37 Emulate Dorcas
38 "Too __": Porter on Sumatra
42 Lilly of pharmaceuticals
43 Held or Christie
45 Dumbbell
46 Modernist
47 Maxims
51 Tenting appurtenance
53 Porter on penthouse elevators
57 Modern art
58 Transgress
59 Mother of the Titans
60 Cachet
62 Cote sound
63 Porter on Detroit or Decatur
66 Kin of et al.
67 "__ million years!"
68 Designer of note
69 Herbert Hoover was one
70 Chaplet
71 Carpenter and soldier

DOWN

1 87 qts. of cranberries
2 Designer Cassini
3 "Get __": Porter on bail-jumping
4 Do some cobbling
5 ". . . man is not __": Pope
6 Kind of window
7 N Japanese city
8 Indian bigwigs
9 Actress Blake
10 One of Rockne's Four Horsemen
11 Cookout favorite
12 McNichols, e.g.
13 Clemson footballer
18 Dangerous
24 Fishgarth
25 Dakota Indian
26 Roberto's residence

27 Floyd won it in '86
28 Sweet one of song
32 Objective
34 "Don't __": Porter on claustrophobia
35 Grocery item
36 Watts event: 1965
39 German cheer
40 Harem room
41 Love apple
44 Thus: Sp.
48 Throat ailment

49 "__ earth?" (incredulity phrase)
50 Nap
52 Russian newspaper
53 Insurgent
54 Steamed
55 Sky Dragon
56 Cod or haddock
60 Contract feat
61 Gunpowder was one
64 Methyl ending
65 Many wks. and mos.

ACROSS

1 Tadzhik and Uzbek: Abbr.
5 Step, in Pau
8 Jewish month
12 Reached or bribed
13 Module
15 __ a customer
16 Words of disapproval
17 Like the latest employee
19 Wear for Astaire
20 Petermen's targets
21 Watson or Weiskopf
22 Tops
24 Fills the suitcase anew
28 Treadle
30 Pulitzer Prize novelist: 1958
32 Nanette preceders
33 Pressure, to an E.E.
34 Wilson hit: 1941
37 Put in one's __ (meddle)
38 Flesh: Comb. form
40 Part of a basilica
41 Chic
43 Pre-premiere events
45 Forgo the diner
47 Aves. and blvds.
48 Former A's infielder Sal
50 Ischia neighbor
53 Anton and Stallone, to friends
57 Hubbub
59 Idaho city
60 Talus
61 Eggs on
62 Adam and Jacob followers
63 Potential capts.
64 Payment, in Passau

DOWN

1 Loudness units
2 Cook two ways
3 Almond liqueur
4 Aquatic insect
5 Disdain, vocalized
6 Chinese seaport city
7 Warm Springs, for one
8 __ Islands in the Bay of Bengal
9 Challenge
10 Blue dye
11 Lines on A.A.A. maps
12 Angular: Comb. form
13 Paley's network
14 Successful
18 August hrs.
21 __ off (angry)
23 Squawks
24 Taylor or Adorée

25 React to love bug
26 Wood burl
27 Kind
28 Pain in the neck
29 "Cielo __"
31 Word with tank or range
35 Dobbin's dish
36 Byzantium, now
39 O.K. and others
42 One of the Philippines

44 City NE of Venice
46 Org. for Belli
49 Comic Ole __
50 French vintner's shed
51 Tia or tante
52 Pom's Chinese rival
53 Bathgate native
54 Cineraria
55 Logo of 13 Down
56 Kind of man
58 Type of agt.

ACROSS

1 TV's "The __"
6 Aid an arsonist
10 Blazer
14 Jeune __
15 Ancient Asian
16 Jason's ship
17 Exhausted
18 Pub drinks
19 __ accompli
20 Eating place
22 She: Fr.
23 Midge
24 Respect
26 Ducks
30 Put on
32 Sequential scale notes
33 Icelandic work
35 Set up
39 N.H. product
41 Robust walker
43 Fabric for a bride
44 Cigar ending
46 Scenarist James
47 Pacific island republic
49 Evaluate
51 Club
54 Santa Anita event
56 Baltic Sea feeder
57 Eating place
63 Starchy edible root
64 Recess at Notre Dame
65 __ acids
66 Sailor's saint
67 "__ Out of My Head," 1964 hit
68 Metal pin
69 Bridge score
70 Nine: Comb. form
71 Peerless plowman

DOWN

1 Out yonder
2 Favus
3 Building wings
4 Finished a sky dive
5 Household
6 Soprano Lucine
7 Detained
8 Paradise
9 Tried out
10 Eating places
11 Papal vestment
12 Brisk
13 Indian pole
21 Not solidified
25 Litigant
26 Energy units
27 Actress Miles
28 She loves: Lat.
29 Eating place
31 U.S. cartoonist
34 Bambi, e.g.

32 Book by Nabokov
34 Hubs
35 Short, light prose work
36 Scdimcnts
37 Tipster's activity
38 Essence
39 Lithe
40 Pittsburgh footballer

42 Squanders
44 Mounts for knights
46 Faint hue
47 Film's Von Stroheim
50 Headcheese, e.g.
53 Minerva, for one
55 Pronoun for a calico cat
56 Stitch

ACROSS

1 Object
5 Hijack
8 Glut
12 Enticed
14 Kimono sash
15 Papal vestment
16 Concur
17 Pirates
19 Symbols in music
21 Piggery
22 Very long time
23 Calendar abbr.
24 This, that or the other
25 Acid
27 Monk's title
30 Cuckoopint
34 Kind of skirt
35 Garland
36 Weapons
37 Items kept on a cushion
42 C.I.A. predecessor
43 Violently frenzied
44 Loop loopers
45 Presidential nickname
46 Burns's word for tiny
47 Hint
50 Houseleek or ground ivy
55 Minor in importance
56 Rosy red dye
57 Urges
58 River in Scotland
59 Roofing material
60 High grade
61 Above, in poesy
62 God of war

DOWN

1 Tumbler
2 Should, with "to"
3 Deck out
4 Villain's look
5 Kind of numeral
6 Port on the Firth of Lorne
7 Celtic star
8 Former V.I.P. of Egypt
9 French writer Claude __
10 Rocky peaks
11 Tintinnabular trio
13 Rely
15 Points on which levers turn
18 In a state of entanglement
20 Certain beans
24 Dry
25 Kind of preview
26 Norse god
27 Alpine snowfield
28 Units of radiation
29 Onager
30 Falsehoods
31 Wallet fillers
32 And

138

33 Platform
34 JKL followers
38 Namesakes of Rebekah's brother: Gen. 24:29
39 Edit; correct
40 Half: Prefix
41 Locales; sites
45 Positive electrode
46 More timid
47 Actor Romero
48 Join
49 Anglo-Saxon serfs
50 Leander's beloved
51 Business-school subj.
52 Wall decoration
53 Hudson Bay Indian
54 Nut used in flavoring
55 Vichy, e.g.

ACROSS

1 One of the Channel Islands
5 Aegean island
10 Caribbean island
14 Kind of code
15 Siouan language
16 "E pluribus __"
17 Curse
18 Bill
19 ". . . in corpore __"
20 Tahiti's former name
22 Authorized agent
24 Legal minorities
25 Short snorts
26 Diatonic notes
27 Skirt style
28 Some eau
31 Airborne biters
34 Dry out
36 A Turner
37 Where Petruchio wived wealthily
38 City in Hawaii
39 Monte Corno's milieu
41 European iris
42 Teeter-totter's Marjorie
43 Cereal of the frisky
44 Former Brit. colonies
45 Broadway's Tommy __
46 Danish island
50 Either of a Bahamian duo
53 Arch's sine qua non
54 Oar shaft
55 Kind of fence
57 Volcanic crater
58 Aware of, as a hoax
59 Pangloss, e.g.
60 Dog star
61 Ring great
62 Harsh
63 Gun for Tommy Atkins

DOWN

1 Wore
2 Muse for Marvell
3 Provide new crew
4 First hit by Rodgers-Hart
5 Cinema
6 Utters
7 Give off coherent light
8 Cry of surprise
9 Cagliari is its capital
10 Tooth prominences
11 Two-toed sloth
12 Batter's ploy
13 Island west of Taiwan
21 Sponsorship
23 "Beowulf," e.g.
25 Exertion
27 Some ancient Iranians
28 Wildcat's pad
29 Gudrun's victim
30 Ancient name of a Cyclades island

31 All smiles
32 Calif. wine area
33 Again
34 "La Vita Nuova" poet
35 Indian Ocean island
37 Nero and Rubinstein
40 Speech part
41 Nocturnal raptors
44 Bavaria, to Berliners

45 Indonesian island
46 Reek
47 Melba or French
48 Growing outward
49 Showed on TV once more
50 Daub
51 Hebrides island
52 Speck
53 Inflate a check
56 __-in-Bay, Ohio

ACROSS

1 The Bard's river
5 Mollycoddle
9 Big, stupid guy
13 Muscovite
14 Switch extender
15 Muscle power
16 Ego behind the plate?
18 Lobster trap
19 Plentifully
20 Gave relief
22 "__ pro nobis"
23 River of Flanders
25 Like some heroes
29 Quonsets
30 Make sure little Irene gets to Iowa, initially?
31 Dried root of a Mexican vine
34 Earth
36 Life, in Udine
37 St. John's or Penn. State
38 Type of note or number
39 Sacred symbol
40 Jambalaya ingredient
41 Six: Comb. form
42 Had significance
43 Ego does some tailing?
45 Quid, in Dogpatch
47 Type of fishing boat
48 Durability
49 Matheson or Conway
52 Arctic sight
54 Capital of S.D.
56 Musical syllables
59 Retain a charged particle?
61 "Hasta luego"
62 Calcium oxide
63 Without
64 Match; equal
65 Business abbr.
66 City in southern Tex.

DOWN

1 Adversario opposite
2 Substitute; deputy
3 Fla. citrus center
4 Org. created in 1949
5 Directive
6 Actress Meyers
7 Chef, at times
8 Hindu discipline
9 Book by an aviculturist?
10 "__-and-Twenty": Johnson
11 Kin of omega
12 He gives a hoot
15 Stormy encounter
17 Praise
21 Finished kid
24 Abstain from
26 City on the Mohawk
27 "__ your life!"
28 Hudson film
29 Be ready to give a black bird?

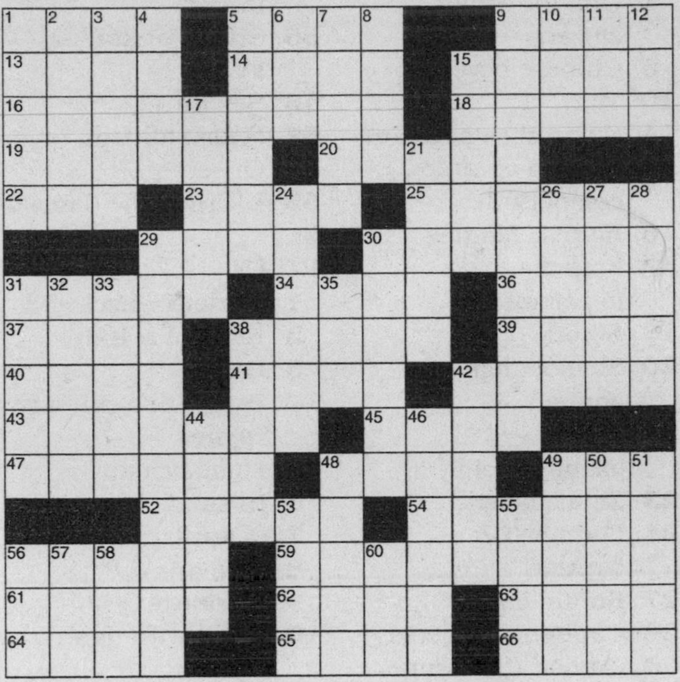

30 Console
31 Prudent beginning
32 Aromatic flavoring
33 African antelope
35 Bagel topper
38 Convolution
42 Dancer Tallchief
44 "The Ballet Class" painter
46 Come into being
48 "__ me!"
49 Error's partner
50 Actor Jeremy
51 Intellectuals' group
53 A neighbor of Ark.
55 Start of the Bay State motto
56 Exhaust
57 "__ to Simplicity": Collins
58 Hammarskjöld's predecessor
60 Trio in summertime

ACROSS

1 Org. for senior citizens
5 Chinese beverage
10 Tizzy
14 Colorful signalman?
15 Certain organic compounds
16 Actress Montez
17 French department
18 Styptic
20 She lost her charges
22 Minute examination
23 Zeta chaser
24 Former N.Z. denizen
27 Koran, e.g.
29 Captious gardener
30 City on the Ganges
31 A son of Poseidon
33 Legendary versifier
35 Meadow lowlands
37 Throw for __
38 Reich salute
39 Salzfleisch
43 Ache
44 Govt. agency
47 Chew noisily
48 Seafaring lad
50 Elegant fabric
53 Corporation
54 Former Ugandan leader
55 Shafts or stalks: Fr.
56 Sea bird
57 Short; abrupt
58 Onset
59 D'Urberville damsel

DOWN

1 Harlot in Ezek. 23
2 River of N Italy
3 Lease
4 Parrot in a nursery rhyme
5 Huge beasts
6 In single file
7 __ sapiens
8 Flee to a J.P.
9 Attribute
10 Word with dash or stick
11 Add up
12 Hebrew high priest
13 U.S. Army branch
19 Sri Lanka export
21 Like a grebe's toes
24 Partner
25 What Cortes coveted
26 Author Rand
28 Island off New Guinea
29 Arachnophobe

31 Machinist's equipment
32 Platforms
33 Large conduit
34 More vitreous
35 Retiring
36 Like Willie Winkie
40 Complete
41 Oak seeds
42 Students' essays
44 Food fish
45 Encourages a thief
46 __ omen (mild invocation)
48 Baseball maneuver
49 Ascetic practice
50 Moccasin
51 Australian ratite
52 Expose

ACROSS

1 Eastern nanny
5 Fibs
10 Surface measure
13 Singer Falana
14 Idolize
15 __ noire
17 Guests of
   62 Across
   stay here
19 Small flats
20 Prefix for type
21 Locofoco, e.g.
23 Dregs
25 Gush forth
26 Inflexible
29 T.E.D. opponent
32 Pompous ones
35 Soon
36 Mrs. Andrew
   Jackson
38 Allhallows __
39 Overlay
40 Soap or horse
   chaser
41 Cold spell
42 Chemical ending
43 Mourner
44 "__ Small World"
45 Skin layer
47 Billy __ Williams
48 __ Bryant Ford
49 Himalayan plant
51 Nestor

53 Stump
57 Schell and
   Muldaur
61 Attend Abbot
62 Medal of Freedom
   awarders
64 Actress Jeffreys
65 Bathes
66 Entrance
67 Depot abbr.
68 Signs
69 Deprivation

DOWN

1 Celebrants' robes
2 Shed
3 Wings
4 This may recede
5 Lake in the Sierra
   Nevada
6 Fuss
7 Boisterous
8 Gaelic
9 Appears
10 Crude calculator
11 Exemplifies
12 Kett of comics
16 Part of i.e.
18 Oboist's purchase
22 Girasol
24 Molded
26 Wingy
27 Vacant
28 Polity

30 Backdrop
31 Treys
33 Widened at the top
34 Calyx part
36 Caviar
37 Auricle
41 Astral
43 River in NW Iran
46 Made a cartograph
48 Zounds!

50 Two: Comb. form
52 Wrongly
53 Auditor, for short
54 English composer
55 Chickpea
56 Firn
58 __-European
59 Panay people
60 Concordes
63 Indonesian coin

ACROSS

1 Cicatrix
5 __ San Lucas, Baja Calif.
9 Earthy pigment
14 Hardy cabbage
15 Waves, at 5 Across
16 English county
17 News, to Sun City editor John B. Bogart
20 Dried up
21 Place for the birds
22 Lou Hoover, __ Henry
23 Trig
25 Wire nail
28 Monetary unit in S. Africa
31 Rental agreement
35 Decay
36 Gudrun's husband
37 Defects
38 Life, to lyricist Lew Brown
41 Certain substances
42 Ship's wheel
43 Spelling event
44 Commemorative stone
45 Order to a broker
46 Bothers
47 Annoying sound in a kitchen
49 Likely
51 Hebrew A
54 Measuring thicknesses
60 Man, to Aristotle
62 Steeple
63 At any time
64 Equal
65 Ruhr city
66 Take five
67 Kind of jerk

DOWN

1 Slide precariously
2 Place to have a "cuppa"
3 Word of regret
4 Stimulate recall
5 Pieces for Pinchas Zukerman
6 Goya's duchess
7 Chum, e.g.
8 Belgian city
9 C.I.A.'s predecessor
10 Montand or Aznavour
11 Conceal
12 A friend of Antony
13 Mil. group
18 One-spot card
19 Dutch commune
24 Morning sound
25 Nerve
26 Mechanical man
27 Latin American gruel
29 TV sitcom
30 Special place

32	Pretext, possibly	50	Corral
33	Structural material	51	Cathedral section
34	Mississippi quartet	52	Cuts, with "off"
36	Tree of the birch family	53	Yalies
37	Went to pieces	55	Bathe
39	Sheet lightning	56	Islands in the Seine
40	Loki's daughter	57	Novel by Ramon José Sender
45	Typewriter bar	58	Appellation
46	In danger	59	Mirth
48	Here, to Henri	61	X, to Cicero

ACROSS

1 __ Raton, Fla.
5 Bay of Naples isle
10 Hostess's request, initially
14 Pronto: Abbr.
15 N.Y. city on the Allegheny
16 Asian ruler
17 Buckles
19 __ doble (corrida music)
20 Two trios and a single
21 One-handed a liner
23 Peace goddess
26 In the past, in the past
27 Grazed
30 Batista's 1959 successor
33 Follower of Paul or Ann
34 Herbs
36 Creek
37 John Wayne's "__ Bravo"
38 Postulation
40 Smith and Jolson
41 Urchin
42 Keepsake
43 CCXCIII x VII
44 Instructive example
46 Colorful thorny hybrids
49 Belt ornament

50 To be, in Toledo
51 Hindered
54 Piece of news
58 Six-stringed instrument
59 The king's brew?
62 Neighbor of Sask.
63 Beethoven's "Für __"
64 Blazing star
65 Photo-finish margin
66 Get the soap out
67 Ash holder

DOWN

1 Fish voice?
2 Italian innkeeper
3 Find fault
4 Calcium phosphate mineral
5 Whirlybird, for short
6 Neighbor of Tenn.
7 According to
8 Informers
9 Scrutinizes
10 Enact anew
11 Computerized streetcars?
12 Jawed grip
13 Stir
18 Machu Picchu's locale
22 Expunge
24 Landing post
25 Descendant of Esau
27 Thin ice, e.g.
28 "Once upon __"

29 Stain repellent's claim?

31 Moon valley

32 Refuge for Bedouins

35 Wild and Elmer

38 Supercilious

39 Fat worker

43 Caustic in manner

45 Monumental stones

47 Churchill's successor as P.M.: 1945

48 Symbol of thinness

51 Terrible ruler

52 Origin of the Louvre's Venus

53 Specialty-food store

55 Borodin's prince

56 Gulf of Finland feeder

57 Gloomy

60 Vodka's rival

61 Nitwit

ACROSS

1 Dross
5 Poplar tree
10 Unruly child
14 Jot
15 Fur scarf
16 Painter Magritte
17 Gathering at the White House
20 Bishopric
21 Balzac's "Le __ Goriot"
22 Blunt; diminish
23 Chianti, e.g.
24 "Sustineo __," U.S.A.F. motto
25 Terrified
28 Thrilling
32 Anxieties
33 Gordon of comics
34 Stir
35 __ Gemayel, former Lebanese President
36 What quibblers split
37 __ Sedgwick, tragic heiress
38 Light Horse Harry
39 Author of "Jude the Obscure"
40 Coop group
41 Triple __: 1882–1915
43 New Orleans eleven
44 Uncivil
45 Nine: Comb. form
46 Sends a check
49 Let it stand
50 Kin of aves.
53 Presidential address
56 Actor Jacques __
57 Wisdom tooth, e.g.
58 Anabaena or nostoc
59 Rubber trees
60 Material for 36 keys
61 Betty __, cartoon flapper

DOWN

1 Tastes
2 Learning
3 Fit to __
4 Argon, e.g.
5 Rise
6 Mart part
7 Southern bread
8 Sprite
9 Unnecessary
10 Kind of bone
11 Sunder or splinter
12 Suffix with resist
13 Kett contemporary
18 Certain moles
19 Attain
23 Small songbird
24 Wing-shaped
25 La __, opera house
26 Tylopod
27 Arabian gazelle
28 Omit
29 Radioactive element

30 Dostoyevsky's "The __"
31 Some Princetonians
33 Burlesque
36 Like Apollo
37 One of five on a map
39 __ couture (high fashion)
40 African language
42 Optical inflammation

43 Scornful
45 Frome of fiction
46 Alphabetic quartet
47 Kin of etc.
48 Best at chess
49 French battle site in W.W. II
50 Missile's home
51 A neighbor of Ghana
52 Lead-pipe cinch
54 Little pocket
55 Capture

ACROSS

1 Southern Slav
6 Addis __
11 Sword cases
13 Emote
15 Barracks gag
16 Obviousness
17 Ending for super
18 Strength
20 Bank book abbr.
21 On a cruise
23 Carry on
24 Prop for Chaplin
25 Zoo attractions
27 Summer on the Seine
28 Lope and pace
29 Commemorative pillar
31 What Junior runs
33 River basin
35 Shards
37 North or Hardy
40 Rub
41 Alias
43 Conductor Koussevitzky
45 Honey factory
46 Terms of a sale
47 Tumult
48 Keelbill
49 Frocks
52 Day, in Durango
53 Annuitant
55 He lives for love

57 Prayers
58 Results when juice is reduced
59 Finnish bath
60 Abounds

DOWN

1 Selects
2 Withdrawal
3 Lout
4 At the peak
5 Norse god
6 Stop, to a sailor
7 They're taken at Vegas
8 "We __ the World"
9 Symbol of minimal help
10 Stresses
11 Islamic sect
12 Fifth Avenue sight
13 Starters
14 Sorts
19 Gear for an aquatic sport
22 Menhaden
24 Egg inspector
26 Frederick Douglass was one
28 Manxmen
30 Eris's brat
32 Greek ar
34 Blackboard adjuncts
35 Black eyes

154

36 Eugene O'Neill heroine
38 Metal used for points of gold pens
39 Selfish ones
40 Coochie-coochie girl
42 Hafez al __, Syrian President
44 States, to Stephanie

46 Scene of the action
49 "Winter's Tale" lord
50 Issue forth
51 "__ achieve greatness . . .": Shak.
54 Houston inst.
56 Sterlet delicacy

ACROSS

1 Molière's forte
6 Blemish
10 Woodwind
14 Less green
15 Martyr of 1776
16 "Little Nell" cartoonist
17 Old World lizard
18 __ and terminer
19 Pre-"Hundred Days" island
20 Marin medium
22 Sale caveat
23 Palo __
24 Rococo
26 Venetian bridge
30 "An __ Day": Longfellow
32 Sight from Taormina
33 Kind of biscuit
35 Tenth part
39 Fifth fingers
41 Kurdish or Pashto
43 Scoff
44 Gram header
46 City on the Humboldt
47 Winds
49 Scottish scones
51 Cottage __
54 Ant. of diminuendo
56 Shofar
57 Some echinoderms
63 The Cornish Wonder: 1761–1807
64 Pointers
65 Scottish theologian: 1810–76
66 Ukrainian capital
67 "__ Tu," 1932 song
68 A family-tree apple
69 She, in Salerno
70 Furbish anew
71 Out on a limb

DOWN

1 Stalemate
2 Latvian capital
3 Give __ on the back (praise)
4 Same, in Strasbourg
5 Mount in Genesis
6 Fire
7 Shuttle's capacity
8 Chromo
9 Panic
10 Its cabins aren't rustic
11 Corkwood
12 Range of influence
13 Expunge
21 A "Fatal Attraction" star
25 "Rio __," 1942 film
26 Agts.
27 Take __ stride
28 Mirthful Meara
29 Montreux locale
31 Bucket's kin
34 Bone: Comb. form

156

36 Cultivate
37 Codling
38 Slaughter of Cooperstown
40 Keogh relatives: Abbr.
42 Allude
45 Leaked out
48 Flatt of bluegrass
50 Acclivity
51 Blow a short putt

52 Ariz. tribe
53 Neighbors of the Hurons
55 __ Japanese War
58 Hibernia
59 Crystal Gayle's trademark
60 __ fixe
61 Promenade des Anglais site
62 Rate, in tennis

ACROSS

1 Boston __ Orchestra
5 Okla. Indian
10 Cloudlike aggregation
14 Tree __ (quiver tree)
15 Early Soviet leader
16 Rialto org.
17 Author Uris
18 Sea duck
19 __-do-well
20 Hardwood tree
22 Trees that grow in wetlands
24 Quebec's Levesque
25 Culture medium
26 Slow down
29 Make-believe
33 Seth's mother
34 Singer Haggard
36 African antelope
37 The 4077th, for short
39 Ranch, in "Giant"
41 King of rug
42 Runs in neutral
44 Concerning
46 Haw. instrument
47 Cooperative effort
49 Oxford's river
51 Porsena of Clusium
52 Gunlock catch
53 Type of nut tree
56 Tree that yields a yellow dye
60 This (girl), to Galba
61 "Romola" author
63 Bird-feeder treat
64 Russian city
65 Annual income, in Arles
66 Budget, in Berlin
67 Some votes
68 Kraut preceder
69 Pianist or fiddler

DOWN

1 Tropical tree
2 Olive genus
3 "Winnie-the-__"
4 A spouse in Sevilla
5 Poisonous shrub
6 Net on a schooner
7 Williams or Griffith
8 Give, in Glasgow
9 Infuriate
10 Lathe spindles
11 Arrow poison
12 Suffix with young or old
13 Sticky substances
21 Bacterium
23 Recent
25 Valor
26 Pardon
27 Dodge
28 Induction-motor inventor
29 Platform part
30 Old Testament book

158

31 Racer, e.g.
32 Flanges
35 Raises
38 Trees used in tanning
40 Sticky-tongued mammal
43 Graceful bird
45 "__ she blows!"
48 Mandates
50 Gone up

52 Struck
53 Nautical cry
54 Like some excuses
55 Big butte
56 Indigenous Japanese
57 Stringed instrument
58 Norman of TV
59 Lyrist Harbach
62 Grassland

ACROSS

1 Complain
5 Converse
9 Topgallants
14 Completed
15 City in W Finland
16 Skiing heights for René
17 Verne's skipper
18 Type of price
19 Sal Maglie was one
20 Wilder's "town"
23 Minks' relatives
24 Atlantic bird
25 Prefix with center
27 Marsh plants
29 Expressed
31 Pindar was one
34 "Of __ I Sing"
35 Snoozed
39 V.P. under G.R.F.
40 Yorkshire city
41 Whetstone
42 Pinza in "South Pacific"
44 An insecticide
47 "Pathetique" or "Moonlight"
51 Suffix with peon or break
52 __ Nellie (prude)
55 Lead sulfide
57 Finn's hideout
60 Star of "M"
61 Secular
62 Secondhand
63 Diaphanous
64 "__ long way to Tipperary . . ."
65 Reno word
66 Llama's milieu
67 Line a roof
68 Word for an école coed

DOWN

1 The Ubangi joins it
2 Wards off
3 Kind of control
4 Put to the test
5 Ran, as a stream
6 Attila's men
7 Rabbit follower
8 Private teacher
9 It always attracts
10 "It's a sin to tell __"
11 ". . . woodman, __ beechen tree!": Campbell
12 Kind of bike
13 Heathrow arrival
21 Rye fungus
22 Dispensers of T.L.C.
26 July 15, e.g.
28 __ qua non
30 Gormandized
32 Penrod's friend

33 The diamond's Speaker

35 Anagram for Ashe

36 Fictional Silver

37 Made beloved

38 __ diem

40 Horne and Nyman

43 Reasonable

45 Press adjuncts

46 Constantine's birthplace

48 Refer to

49 Raise a nap

50 Temper

53 Mulligrubs

54 On Mom's side

56 Confuse

58 Hudson Bay Indian

59 Amigo's agreement

60 Pharm. degree

ACROSS

1 Digest, for short
6 Goodbye, London style
10 "__ Ideas," 1951 song
14 Irregular
15 Middle East gulf
16 Fountain order
17 "__ Boccanegra," Verdi opera
18 U.S.A. or the former U.S.S.R.
20 High schoolers, usually
22 Actress MacMahon
23 Ice palace?
24 Acclamation
26 Key spot on a car
30 Allergic disorder
33 Tiny
34 Like some beer
36 Pertaining to the east
37 Ticket booth sign
38 Fire preceder
39 Press closing
40 College in N.C.
42 Craft, in Cordoba
43 "Music" to a hitchhiker
45 Octogenarian's goal
47 Bothered continually
49 Clean a blackboard
51 Ski resort in Utah
52 Unexpected loss
54 Goofed on the diamond
59 Crescent-shaped roll
61 Form or talk ending
62 De __, "The Green Pastures"
63 Actress Tushingham
64 Meaning
65 Author Rand et al.
66 "Thanks __!"
67 Garden implement

DOWN

1 Remainder
2 Clinton's canal
3 Inherit
4 "__ Born," 1948 Kaye musical
5 Offside result
6 Story
7 Hebrew month
8 On edge
9 Ampersand
10 Set apart
11 Be completely self-evident
12 Earl of Avon
13 Anagram for 42 Across
19 Buddies
21 W Afr. republic
25 Part of T.L.C.
26 Creator of Hedda Gabler
27 "The __ Left Behind Me"

162

28 Singular person
29 Below, to Byron
31 Actress Eva __ Saint
32 Make __ of (finish off)
35 Befuddled
38 The Keys are these
41 Nymphs of the deep
43 Dyeing ester
44 Propertied
46 Uses a shuttle
48 What some hoods beat

50 Computer communications, for short
52 Bruins' home
53 Importune
55 Division word
56 Photo finish
57 Bacchanalian cry
58 Author Earl __ Biggers
60 Srta.'s mother

ACROSS

1 "__ be praised!"
6 Word with land or sea
11 F.D.R. agency
14 The huntress
15 Actress Marta
16 Cry of triumph
17 "Shoot, if you must, this __": Whittier
19 Guidonian note
20 Writing implement
21 Aware of
22 High priest
23 Lend
25 Moslem mendicant monk
27 Conception
30 N.Y. time in May
31 Ponies
32 "¡__ bueno!"
33 Pert
35 Mil. branch
36 "A __ man speaking to men": Wordsworth
38 Utility must
42 Solti's title
43 __ Islands of Denmark
45 Citrus drink
46 Tea fare
48 Gerona's river
49 Kind of appeal
50 Attics
51 Maximally
53 Abate
54 African fox
56 Addison's partner
60 Goethe's "The __ King"
61 "Her __ . . .": Coleridge
63 Kind of cross
64 Growing out
65 Turkish decree
66 Compass pt.
67 Hearing, e.g.
68 "__ Is Born"

DOWN

1 Fusses
2 Cadence
3 Slipper preceder
4 England, to Caesar
5 __-scarum
6 Pen
7 Associates
8 "__ we all?"
9 Irish fuel
10 "Till the __," 1945 song
11 "Barefoot boy, with __!": Whittier
12 __ a day
13 Runs a meeting
18 Former Turkish coins
24 Turn __ ear to

164

26 "Rule, Britannia"
man
27 Demon
28 Twosome
29 "Five foot two, __"
33 Bargain events
34 Oda site
37 Dye
39 Sad
40 Tokyo, once
41 Johnny __
44 Swears to

46 Rains icy
particles
47 Mongoose targets
49 Pilots
51 "A life's but __":
Shak.
52 Groove
55 __ qua non
57 Part of Q.E.D.
58 Castor's mother
59 German river
62 Tiny

ACROSS

1 Pt. of speech
4 Conductor Dorati
9 Arm, in Armentières
13 Condemn
15 Greenstreet's screen pal
16 Sunday section, for short
17 "__ Karenina"
18 Chicago's Rumanian-born conductor
20 Secure
22 Philadelphia's Ormandy
23 Court notable
24 Drab color: Ger.
25 Main artery
27 Org. of 26 Down
29 Vice __
33 Underworld kingpin
34 Strauss's "The Blue __"
36 Like Joe Miller jokes
37 Spanish name for an Iberian river
38 Edwin Booth's milieu
39 In __ way (seriously ill)
40 Honolulu beach
41 Orchestrated
42 Dream, in Dijon
43 Saint-Saens "La __ Macabre"
45 Composer Rorem
46 Valuable violin
47 Gabor and Le Gallienne
49 Locked
50 Cherished

53 Jazz conductor-musician Oscar __
57 New York's Indian-born conductor
59 State where Szell conducted
60 Relative of the buffalo
61 Friendship
62 Cellar contents
63 English conductor Boyd __
64 City near Warren, Ohio
65 Tintern Abbey's river

DOWN

1 G. Eliot's "__ Bede"
2 Lady of Lisbon
3 Berlin's conductor Herbert __
4 Seaweeds
5 Negative votes
6 Pony
7 Timetable abbr.
8 Postimpressionist painter
9 Coarse shoe
10 Part
11 Memo abbr.
12 Silk, in Lyon
14 Man at the podium
19 Debonair
21 Kind of housing loan: Abbr.
24 Overcharged
25 Trod the boards
26 Manchurian-born conductor Seiji
27 Conductors' implements

166

28 Kind of drum
30 Atlanta's conductor
31 Conductor Rostropovich's nickname
32 Subjoined
34 Mil. decoration
35 Foundation
39 Toscanini and others
41 "__ Days in May"
44 Describes certain modern music
46 Haggard title

48 Madison Ave. type
49 Corset appurtenances
50 Moslem call to prayer
51 Sahara feature
52 Orchestra member
53 Conductor Spitalny of yesteryear
54 Wagon or kitchen ending
55 Unctuous
56 Score feature
58 __ Koussi, peak in Chad

ACROSS

1 Recorded, in a way
6 Site of Port-au-Prince
11 Delay, old style
12 Past month
14 Man from Oman, e.g.
15 Delicious drinks
17 Hornswoggled
18 Bush. or pk.
20 Navajo's home
21 Utah's __ National Park
22 Eyelid inflammations
24 Rama's wife
25 Superlative suffix
26 Scottish royal family: 1371–1714
28 January 1 drink
29 Loses hope
31 Swimming mammals
33 Famed octogenarian
34 Malay boat
35 Tex. river
38 They get lots of suits
42 "To __ is human . . .": Pope
43 Makes beloved
45 A nephew of Abraham
46 Low-skilled worker
48 Sights on a jalopy
49 Commanded
50 Christie and Karenina
52 Posed
53 Eton boy's mom
54 Milk sugar
56 Slow disintegration
58 Eagle or lark
59 Relative magnitudes
60 Viewpoint
61 Luster

DOWN

1 Sites of small tempests
2 Vice President Barkley
3 Indemnified
4 Airport abbr.
5 Render alcohol unfit for drinking
6 TV detective
7 October __
8 Constant desire
9 Schipa and Gobbi of opera
10 Picture in the mind
11 Injury
13 Skilled speaker
14 Dressed timber roughly
16 Hidden hindrances
19 An orangutan
22 Salary
23 Squirrels and magpies
26 Rhone tributary

27 Porticoes

30 Greek letter

32 Dress leather

34 Large serving dishes

35 Flower part

36 Punta __, Chilean port

37 Wild ones at 40 Down

38 "Last Supper" picture

39 High spirits

40 Western jamborees

41 Ship's rear

44 Abandon

47 Province of South Africa

49 Memorable bandleader

51 Marsh bird

53 Speck

55 Cambodian coin

57 Stadium sound

ACROSS

1 This may turn
5 Help a hood
9 Senseless?
13 Eye layer
14 Plant life
15 To you, Pierre!
16 Pupil's ordeal
17 Happy as __
18 Lizard: Comb. form
19 L.A. campus
20 Small opening
21 Used acid
23 Ab successor
25 Labor safety org.
26 Doubleday and Li'l
28 Amanda of "A Year in the Life"
32 Fall asleep
33 Like a paleface?
34 To, in Dundee
35 Algerian port
36 Rajah's wife
38 Simon-__ (authentic)
39 Rather
40 This can put you in a bind
41 Feathered
43 What daredevils go to
45 Kappa chaser
46 Participial endings
47 Russian stream
48 You, right now
51 Round of applause
53 Old French coin
56 Steinbeck migrant worker
57 "__ Came Jones," 1945 movie
59 "Down with le roi!"
60 Jamie who sounds distant
61 Marie Sklodowska __
62 Guitar's cousin
63 Words from the pro group
64 A Gabor and a Peron
65 Mr. Hoople

DOWN

1 Garb for Susan Jaffe
2 Currier's partner
3 Next generation member
4 Tuck away
5 "__ want for Christmas . . ."
6 Lugger or hooker
7 Slip up
8 Bets big
9 Racing acronym
10 A Monument Valley site
11 Grimace
12 Larry of the N.B.A.
14 Loses favor
20 Shoot the curl
22 People generally
24 Ames or Uris
25 Platinum wire loop
26 Positive terminal
27 Shoddy merchandise

170

28 Glazier's wares
29 Inept boxer
30 Displayed scull skill
31 "__ body cry?": Burns
37 Gibraltar denizens
38 Mountain lion
40 Coty or Clair
42 Bedeck
44 Carson's stand-in, once

48 Parlor piece
49 Give the green light
50 Luigi's funds
51 "__ fugit"
52 Flavoring for a Nice cordial
54 First Triumvirate foe
55 Applications
58 Lemmon film: 1967
59 Mode leaders

ACROSS

1 Billiard stroke
6 Track event
10 "Pay attention!"
14 Two of Henry VIII's six
15 "Come __ my parlor"
16 Hyalite
17 Ermine in summer
18 Yannick of tennis
19 Lowest pinochle card
20 Minn. site of large open-pit iron mine
22 Suitcases
24 Grasping
25 Out of control
26 A bee of sorts
30 Lagniappe
34 Similar: Prefix
35 Capp creature
36 Knot up
37 Light up
39 Govt. economist's concern
41 Mongolian wasteland
42 Frenzy
44 City on the Dnepr
47 Tend
48 Revise
49 Summons of a sort
51 Personality influencer
53 An officer and a gentleman?
54 Mason's creator
57 Andrew and Edward

61 "The __ love . . ."
62 Squash
64 Worship
65 Joy ride
66 "__ neighbor and weigh"
67 Composer Ethelbert
68 Suspend
69 Director Fritz
70 Tendency

DOWN

1 Hot Lips starred in this TV hit
2 Opposed
3 One lacking noblesse oblige
4 Tar's gear holder
5 Appropriate to summer
6 Talk tediously
7 Up: Prefix
8 P.O.W. camp
9 Boring
10 Crown colony
11 Samoan port
12 Jingled
13 Swiss painter
21 Shade of green
23 Oodles
26 Greek letter
27 Followers of Mohammed
28 Not a soul
29 __-Poo of "The Mikado"

172

31 Ruth's
   mother-in-law
32 Name of eight
   popes
33 Hurl
38 Blowout
40 Popular game
43 Middle East gulf
45 "The Hungarian
   Rome"
46 Something different

49 Singer Brewer
50 One who might gain
   interest
52 Tibetan neighbor
54 Kin of gee
55 Newspaper org.
56 Check
58 Inlet
59 St. Patrick's land
60 Dispatch
63 Wrestler's objective

ACROSS

1 Goggler
5 Take __ view (be leery)
9 Duffer's nemesis
13 Quit
14 Choler
15 Bindlestiff
16 Spent
17 Dec. 24 and 31
18 Black, in poesy
19 Rock group
21 A la __
22 L.A. gridders
23 Emulates Falstaff
25 Giroux or Greeley
29 Of a bygone era
31 Tureen
32 Part of T.L.C.
34 Actor Tamiroff
37 Taken out
39 Mali neighbor
42 Withered
43 Famed garden
45 Weird
46 Coeur d'__, Idaho
48 Tries
50 Abate
53 Standard
55 With 49 Down, suspense writer
56 Rock group
62 Time __ half
63 Major ending

64 "__ Doone"
65 Threshold
66 Touch not!
67 Rye fungus
68 Peete's props
69 Scuttles
70 Totter

DOWN

1 Broker's order
2 Colombian city
3 D __ dog
4 Tree: Comb. form
5 Nautical location
6 Quotient element
7 "__ a Song Go . . ."
8 Synchronized
9 Rock group
10 Automaton
11 Dwelling
12 Dixie dishes
13 __ Calloway
20 "Comedy of Errors," e.g.
24 Signify
25 Actor Byrnes
26 "__ Irae," ancient hymn
27 Cartographer's dot
28 Rock group
30 __-majesté
33 Arabian gulf

174

35 Translation for Ovid's "obtineo"

36 Night add-on

38 Cast header

40 Kind of blank

41 Belgian-French river

44 Indicated

47 Catch with a net

49 See 55 Across

50 Part of L.C.D.

51 Ford or Pyle

52 Advance furtively

54 "Golden Boy" playwright

57 Football's Graham

58 Knowledge

59 Egg on

60 Organic compound

61 Posed

ACROSS

1 Parties
6 A dollar in Kuwait
11 __ eggs
13 Cotton-wool fabric
15 Middle Eastern state
16 Church official
17 Nasty fellow
18 Moon of the comics
20 Water source
21 City in S France
23 Unites
24 Opening
25 Slow, to Muti
27 __ Chiang, Chinese writer
28 Dorian Gray's creator
29 Library section
31 Keglers' marks
33 Haggard tale
34 Time frame
35 Site of Plato's Academy
38 Equestrian's pace
41 Show disdain
42 Brighton break
44 Ecological cycles
46 Mind
47 Do the honors, at dinner
49 Computer feed
50 Part of i.e.

51 Rutabagas
53 Kin, for short
54 Whatnot
56 Vacationer's delight
58 City in S Ariz.
59 More strict
60 Hews
61 Did carpentry

DOWN

1 Brides, e.g.
2 Clear
3 Shooting match, French style
4 Jack of movies and TV
5 Arrangement
6 Does hose repair
7 Followers: Suffix
8 Zip
9 France of France
10 Impedes
11 Transferred picture
12 Holds off
13 Sights at Oxford
14 Brave's place
19 Links position
22 Hidden, as contraband
24 Stolen
26 Pigment for Picasso

176

28 Alerts
30 Murray or Dryden
32 Pod unit
35 "__ robins . . .": Kilmer
36 Camp accommodations
37 Ogles
38 Quibbles
39 Error indication
40 Sleeping
41 Dutch genre painter
43 Shore flier
45 Tulwar
47 Parish priests, in Paris
48 Kin of fleurets
51 Toxophilite William
52 Hindu deity
55 Sal of songdom
57 Emulate Betsy Ross

ACROSS

1. Gregory Peck role: 1956
5. Siffle
9. Offends
14. Egyptian queen of the gods
15. Stein-Plimpton book
16. Small bay
17. Malay craft
18. Hitchcock's "__ Window"
19. Emporium
20. Skeptic's comment
23. __ fainéant (do-nothing king)
24. Roof adornment
25. Weighty weight
26. Skeptic's seasoning?
32. Bravo or Grande
33. Comic Jay
34. High flier
38. Man is one
40. Swordfish's sword
43. Soul-seller Dorian
44. Cartographer's collection
46. Shade
48. Mamie's mate
49. "Tell it __" (skeptic's comment)
53. Bill's possible future
56. Monk's title
57. Hulk Hogan victory
58. Skeptic
64. Yippie Hoffman
65. Ovid
66. African shrub
68. Defensive ditches
69. Having wings
70. Car part
71. Winter forecast
72. Zeus' spouse
73. Being, to Aquinas

DOWN

1. Viper
2. Spy name
3. Molecule element
4. African secessionist state: 1967–70
5. Juliet and Cordelia
6. Manuscript word
7. "Owa tagu __"
8. Sequence
9. This may be guided
10. Division word
11. Mock
12. Iron: Comb. form
13. Beer mug
21. Muddy the waters
22. Menton is one
26. A Met score
27. Main point
28. Aeronautics maneuver
29. J. Denver's "__ World"
30. Special talent
31. Traffic ticket
35. Smile broadly
36. Actress Veronica
37. The night's thousand

178

39 Ingest
41 Flange
42 Poet's repetition for effect
45 Most compassionate
47 Peter, Paul and Mary, e.g.
50 Cycle beginning
51 Mrs. Van Buren
52 Pokey person
53 Tea Party inciter

54 Computer-language acronym
55 Old Roman trumpets
59 Fall for a trick
60 Strong wind
61 Ivan or Peter
62 "Woe is me!"
63 "My Three __" (TV oldie)
67 Supplement with "out"

ACROSS

1 Prefix with john or god
5 Magna __
10 Norwegian king
14 Ardor
15 "On life's vast __ . . .": Pope
16 Venetian magistrate
17 Storage places
18 Talkative
20 Singer Tennille
21 Actress Joanne
22 Court schedule
23 Lets stand
25 More agreeable
27 Sally
29 ". . . Western Front" novelist
34 Fort Worth inst.
36 Plumber?
38 Some are palookas
39 Skater Heiden
41 Figure of authority
43 Dissolve
44 "Divorce capital," once
45 Pyromaniac's crime
47 Peer at
48 Southwestern shrub
51 Warrant off.
53 Three-time Masters champion
55 Fabled guardian of mines
58 Las Vegas features

62 Soc.-page denizen
64 TV's "L. __"
65 Large area
67 Abundant
68 "Charley's __"
69 Tips
70 Wickedness
71 Don Giovanni, e.g.
72 Robes
73 Something to make

DOWN

1 Liabilities
2 Prufrock's creator
3 Models
4 Locale phrase: Lat.
5 Something too common
6 Type of squash
7 Syllabus material
8 Ala __, Kazakhstani range
9 Garland
10 Of a Pindaric
11 Defunct magazine
12 Malarial fever
13 Weskit
19 Comedienne Witherspoon
24 Taste
26 Proserpina's mother
28 Jay's cousin
30 Indy driver's concern
31 Export from Seville
32 "The __ Duckling"

1	2	3	4		5	6	7	8	9		10	11	12	13
14					15						16			
17					18				19					
20					21				22					
23				24		25		26						
	27			28		29				30	31	32	33
34	35			36		37					38			
39			40		41				42		43			
44						45				46		47		
48				49	50				51		52			
			53				54		55			56	57
58	59	60	61			62		63		64			
65					66					67			
68					69					70			
71					72					73			

33 Punta del __,
Uruguay
34 Part of a school
year
35 Algonquian
language
37 Pentagonal base
40 "Le __ d'Or"
42 Plunder
46 Nailing block
49 Utilities customer
50 Thrips, e.g.

52 Caught
54 Alluvial plain
56 Puzo subject
57 Confederate general
58 Winter Palace
resident
59 __ vitae (alcohol)
60 Rot!
61 Overdue
63 Mamie's
predecessor
66 Out-of-style jacket

ACROSS

1 Defense method
5 Cut capers
10 Wharf
14 "On the land __ the sea"
15 Play girl
16 Biblical preposition
17 JACK
19 "An apple __ . . ."
20 Granada gold
21 "Scarface" star
23 Stop transmitting
27 Flatboats
28 "__ Apart," Frost poem
29 Sternward
32 Israeli Chief of Staff: 1974
35 Made a web
36 Standoffish
37 Nice one
38 Hospital ship
39 "__, thou art sick": Blake
40 Jazz trumpeter Al
41 Botanist Gray
42 A metalworker
43 On the Black
44 Hankering
45 Palette pigment
46 Grating sound
47 Drop off
49 Silly talk
51 Old mild oath
55 Intoxicant in liq.
56 Complete
57 BILL
62 Notation on a ticket
63 Dodge
64 Tick off
65 Pelagic predator
66 Theme of this puzzle
67 Way out

DOWN

1 Shake up
2 Purpose
3 Bandleader Severinsen
4 Basketball defense
5 Live off the __ the land
6 Cell letters
7 Quechua
8 Threshold
9 HARRY
10 Mountebank
11 FRANK
12 __ impasse
13 Cellist Ma
18 Cow poke
22 Pseudo-esthetic
23 Glide
24 Barge in
25 BOB
26 Actress Fawcett

30 Hooch

31 Maintain

33 Delusory

34 One more try on a set

36 JIMMY

40 Uncompromising

42 Big, stupid guy

46 Collected

48 A memorable Nelson

50 Merchandise

51 __ du Nord, Parisian depot

52 Suffix with liquid

53 Pepper plant

54 Canned meat

58 Dutch commune

59 Nope

60 Wallach or Whitney

61 Even though

ACROSS

1 Frosted
5 Actress from Greece
10 Thicke from Canada
14 Ball role
15 In accord
16 Tarzan transporter
17 Temperamental one
19 Room addition
20 Take both sides
21 Arranged by type
23 Invalid
24 Computer device
25 Walk like ducks
28 Opposite of estivated
31 Red as __
32 S.R.O. indications
33 Lingerie item
34 Loving
35 Enclosed
36 Peewee
37 Tsk
38 Solemn
39 Goblin
40 Purist
42 Wakes
43 Unnecessary feature
44 Quaker leader
45 Yacht's home
47 Confuse
51 Author Murdoch
52 Parade
54 Resort for one's niece?
55 Fish locator
56 "Do __ others . . ."
57 Summer refreshments
58 Barbara and Anthony
59 Leave behind

DOWN

1 Little rascals
2 Uncovered wagon
3 Eastern bigwig
4 Insisted on
5 Boat mover
6 Bikini, e.g.
7 Corncake
8 Shirley or Sheridan
9 Spicy
10 Reluctant
11 Highway trashers
12 Pot starter
13 Lack
18 Grown
22 Excuses
24 Clementine's dad, e.g.
25 Floats

184

26 Here and there
27 Toothpaste
28 Sounder
29 "Sesame Street" character
30 Goes with
32 Record-company name
35 Cave in
36 Gathers
38 Cheat

39 Merit pay
41 Crucial times
42 Alludes (to)
44 Southern nut
45 Starling relative
46 Dull
47 Radius, e.g.
48 Actress Merrill
49 Scads
50 Father of Cainan
53 Staff

ACROSS

1 Sounds from Santa
5 Valley
9 Health resort
12 One of a Latin trio
13 Mr. __, minstrel endman
14 Frau's counterpart
15 Mobster's cry in a gunfight
18 Daughter's sib
19 U.S. author James
20 Take the stump
21 One of a pair
22 Snuggles
24 Venetian's neighbor
27 Punishes a schoolboy
28 Excuse
29 Rani's robe
30 Mimic
33 Second mobster's query
37 Gel
38 Optimistic
39 Bellini opera
40 Strike
42 Hones a straightedge
43 Allah is their God
46 Throb painfully
47 Spaces
48 Dies __
49 Royal symbol
52 First mobster's reply

56 Compass points
57 Lock of hair
58 Tardy
59 Clam, at times: Abbr.
60 Italian noble family
61 Took a jet

DOWN

1 Reaps alfalfa
2 Melville novel
3 Actress Goldie
4 Baseball great
5 Dean
6 Heavenly being, to Henri
7 Zodiacal sign
8 Id follower
9 Flower part
10 Talk foolishly
11 Van Gogh painted here
13 Commence
14 Livestock groups
16 Fiftieth state
17 Fashion
21 Bath fixtures
22 Tote
23 One
24 Shoulder enhancers
25 S. African lily
26 Eat sparingly
27 Effect's beginning
29 Injections
30 Hair style
31 Gas-station fixture

32 Greek mil. group of W.W. II

34 Remove excess

35 Song of praise

36 "She __ a Yellow Ribbon"

40 Parts of beds

41 Fit neatly

42 Sings like Fitzgerald

43 Lions' prides

44 Praying figure

45 Drain

46 Hit the deck

48 "__ a Kick Out of You"

49 October birthstone

50 Assess

51 Exploded, as a tire

53 Nice summer

54 Correspondence abbr.

55 Nixie or pixie

ACROSS

1 With 12 Across, old hymn
5 Merganser
9 Race part
12 See 1 Across
13 July 4 event
16 Ratite bird
17 Refuge
18 Confused
19 Scull implement
20 Whenever
22 Divided coin?
24 Macho ones
25 Norwegian coin
27 Chutzpah
28 Grampus
29 Flies, mice, etc.
31 Sebaceous cysts
33 Water or river follower
34 Capuan's country
38 "The __ of St. Agnes"
39 Cloth for sheeting
41 King topper
42 Legendary horse
44 Muscle: Comb. form
45 Sights in Sedan
46 "__ everybody?"
48 Chinese dynasty
49 Overbearing
52 Japanese statesman: 1841–1909
53 Kind of ink

56 Bill for a carpenter?
58 Augusta golf tournament
60 __ in (weary)
61 Bow and Barton
63 Macaws
64 Singer Peggy
65 Beliefs
66 Actor Wilder
67 Rockies time: Abbr.
68 Victim
69 Redact

DOWN

1 A certain Shore
2 Vernon's partner
3 Inherited wealth?
4 Game dogs
5 G.I. ration
6 Reconstructed
7 Kind of shrew
8 Matthau or Scott
9 German Pope: 1049–54
10 Fine fiddle
11 Treasury
14 Morning moisture
15 Descendant of Esau
21 Business abbr.
23 __ fide
26 Russian coin?
30 Currency in Cyprus
31 Arachnid's ambush
32 Stowe tot
33 The Venerable __

188

35 Cleaned filthy lucre?
36 Frozen water
37 Loser to D.D.E.
39 Subject of a TV ad
40 Robots
43 "Rub-__"
45 Kind of point
47 Former Chinese province

48 Towel word
49 Sacred song
50 Chest rattles
51 Baby bird of prey
54 Citizen of Jask
55 Talent or wealth
57 __ Elum, city in Wash.
59 Vice prin.
62 Old car

ACROSS

1 Updike's "The __ Door"
5 Makes a deposit
9 __ a beet
14 Pitchers' stats
15 First; chief: Comb. form
16 Soap plant
17 Gay cadence
18 Glass panel
19 Canadian fliers
20 Golden __
23 Spanish article
24 Kisser
25 East Indian sailor
29 Objects
34 "Or lend __ to Plato . . .": Tennyson
35 County center
36 Jackie's second
37 Silver __
41 Building wing
42 Relaxation
43 Kitchen utensil
44 Devoid of inhabitants
47 Makes a goal
48 Thus, to Virgil
49 School org.
50 Tin __
59 Radiotelephony term
60 Spoken
61 Against
62 Indian, e.g.
63 Play part
64 Examine
65 Approach sideways
66 First sin site
67 Kind of vision

DOWN

1 Addressed or control preceder
2 Integument
3 Stallion, e.g.
4 East, to Juan
5 Loom up
6 Pulls along
7 Lisbon lady
8 Word on a proof
9 A stew
10 Come out
11 Busy one
12 As well
13 Rate a netman
21 Mrs. Schumann
22 Speak theatrically
25 Put on cargo
26 Tropical lizard
27 Joins the bears
28 Golfer Peete
29 "__-porridge hot . . ."
30 Order to a chef
31 Less hazardous

32 Rich find
33 N.H.L. teams
35 Hit a fly
38 Respond to
39 Wilde or Levant
40 Branco or Bravo
45 Pertaining to bone
46 Gothic re-enforcing rib
47 Purloined

49 Family name of American artists
50 N.F.L. players
51 Places
52 Matured
53 Olden times
54 Goad
55 Don't eat
56 Tale opener
57 Emphatic type: Abbr.
58 Occupation

ACROSS

1 Word used when a balloon bursts
5 Ring around the collar?
10 Witticism
14 Within: Comb. form
15 Type of meter
16 "For __ us a child . . ."
17 Maple genus
18 Compound that's a bum steer?
19 Troubles
20 Story by Dr. Seuss
23 Ubangi feeder
24 Q-U connection
25 Places for bouts
28 Fuel gp.
30 Do away with
33 Fountain orders
34 Speaker's stand
35 Grown-up filly
36 Warning to a speeder
39 Cleveland's lake
40 Finished
41 Took steps
42 Mariner's dir.
43 She played Stella Johnson
44 Apt to happen
45 Hood's refresher
46 Item on a social schedule
47 Alice Mitchell's son
55 N.C. college
56 Closely related group
57 Utah park
58 Havoc from Vancouver
59 People who sound inviting
60 __ the finish
61 M.C. Trebek
62 This raises some dough
63 Luncheon ender

DOWN

1 Austin __ State U., Tenn.
2 Halfway to twice
3 Baltic waterway
4 Loren's "The __ Pilgrim"
5 Wall Street category
6 Group with class?
7 Corticotrophin
8 Syngman __ of S. Korea
9 Stronghold
10 Gallon, less 75%
11 Module
12 "__ be a pleasure!"
13 Emulate Carol Alt
21 Rental paper
22 L.A. campus
25 Longs for
26 Bellows
27 Borden bovine
28 Like some buckets
29 Marina mole
30 Tend to the turkey

31 Russian co-op
32 Penurious
34 Parker of baseball
35 Northwest Territorics district
37 In humble fashion
38 He played John Boy's pop
43 One of certain Bulldogs
44 Weakest, as excuses

45 Growing family's requirement
46 Unpaid bills
47 Warwick's "__ Vu"
48 Av successor
49 "__ but the brave . . ."
50 Its bark is silent
51 __ snag (have trouble)
52 "__ Misbehavin' "
53 Ulster, e.g.
54 Grafted, in heraldry

ACROSS

1 Violin precursor
6 Oriental nurse
10 Indian of Peru
14 Muse of poetry
15 Fountain fare
16 Best Actress awardee: 1963
17 Establish a scholarship
18 Type of coat or wind
19 Labor
20 "__ Abner"
21 Excessive wealth
24 Jane __, Henry VIII's third wife
26 Up in the __ (undecided)
27 Excessive wealth
33 Luxurious
36 Disencumber
37 Harem room
38 Northern constellation
39 Nocturnal flier
40 Iberian Peninsula country
42 Actress Rita
43 Any Phoenix N.B.A. player
44 "Tristram Shandy" author
45 Rolling in money
49 Argon, e.g.
50 Sculler
54 Excessive wealth
59 "Death in the Afternoon" cheer
60 Exchange premium
61 Neglect
62 Bring together
64 Vend
65 Kent's friend
66 Stuck in the mud
67 Pay attention
68 Brings to a conclusion
69 Coast Guard women

DOWN

1 Staggers
2 "Sesame Street" character
3 Very much: Colloq.
4 D.D.E.'s command
5 Range riders
6 Toward the back, to Halsey
7 Defensive ditch
8 Mine entrance
9 Sail rope
10 Dr. Salk, once
11 Night light
12 Father of Enoch
13 Helper
22 Dilapidation
23 Singer-actress Zadora
25 Construct
28 Appomattox figure

194

29 Pose
30 Emulate an eagle
31 Host at Valhalla
32 Enclolure
33 Edible starch
34 Where Kerman is
35 Soil conditioner
39 Inge's "__ Stop"
40 Breastbones
41 Fondles
43 Heart contraction
44 Wither

46 Ancient
47 Utter
48 Highways
51 Danccr Shearer
52 Modify
53 Requires
54 Prepare potatoes
55 S-shaped curve
56 Aswan Dam river
57 Arabian sultanate
58 Tie tightly
63 Short snort

ACROSS

1 Designate
4 Dalton, formerly of "Falcon Crest"
8 Hidden explosive
12 A Guthrie
13 Green tint
14 Steve Cram, e.g.
15 Spirit of the sea
17 More slippery
18 Firefighters' instruments
19 Geological ridges
20 Cool cat's cry
21 Aversion
23 __-de-chaussée (ground floor)
24 More nimble
27 Meter preceder
30 Exude
33 Miller's "__ the Fall"
35 Whitney, to Dionne
37 Pindar product
38 Measure of capacity
39 Nurses in the Orient
40 Standard
42 Beatty and Rorem
43 Babbled
45 Prince Valiant's son
47 Make new again
50 Pod preceder
53 Like some cells
56 Do slaloms
58 Morning sound
59 Man in the street
60 Bustles
61 Other: Comb. form
62 "__ and the Swan": Yeats
63 Fencing weapon
64 A loser to Louis
65 Hero chaser

DOWN

1 Refrain syllables
2 Sergeant York
3 First Secretary of Transportation
4 Coat metal
5 Stems of hops
6 Sanctified
7 Sandburg's "The People, __"
8 Loaded cocktail
9 Netter Nastase
10 At no time, to bards
11 Makes a boo-boo
12 First donor?
14 Co-Nobelist in Literature: 1904
16 Ornamental stone
19 Clairvoyance letters
22 Late bloomer
23 Cousin of John Doe
25 Major chaser
26 Willis of N.B.A. fame
27 Miscellany

196

28 Flaccid
29 Kind of drop
31 "__ Cane"
32 Knot-tying words
34 Els, e.g.
36 Respects
41 Toro tempter
44 Goal
46 Porter's Sweeney
48 Four-stringed
   instrument

49 Anoint, once
50 Subway must
51 __ la Paix
52 "__ girl!"
53 Top of the monk
54 Poorly
   proportioned
55 Miami's county
57 Salvador of art
59 Part of a boxer's
   arsenal

ACROSS

1 Arab garment
4 Midler or Davis
9 Charges
13 Swallow greedily
15 Yearned
16 Latin I verb
17 City on the Oka
18 Across: Prefix
19 Very small creature
20 Swift dog
22 Tanker
23 Byelorussian capital
24 Dahl or Francis
25 English county
28 Word of apology
30 Attu native
31 Monster
32 Harvest
36 Large amount
37 Donizetti heroine
38 "Das Rheingold" role
39 Route
40 World-turner
41 Measure of flow of light
42 Island near Naples
44 Silly
45 Defective cars
48 Ruth's mother-in-law
51 Glory
52 Of farm management
56 Other, in Oviedo
57 Resident of 14 Down
58 TV science program
59 Horse color
60 River between Argentina and Uruguay
61 Overcharge
62 Associate
63 President called Old Eight to Seven
64 Santa Fe–to–Taos dir.

DOWN

1 Excited
2 Slayer of Hamilton
3 Opposite of aweather
4 Mehta's need
5 Light brown hues
6 An American festival
7 Incline
8 Begley and Asner
9 Features of 6 Down
10 Rousseau novel
11 Consumed
12 Cubic meter
14 Site of first get-together that led to 6 Down
21 Clue
22 Hockey great
24 Region
25 Moist
26 Lamb coverup
27 Escape hole

29 Alencon is its capital

31 Reputation

33 Writer Bombeck

34 Capital of South Yemen

35 Window part

37 Swiss mountains

41 Draw

43 Hill dweller

45 Arrowsmith's first wife

46 Laud

47 Rivera product

49 Crest on a range

50 Namesakes of Mrs. Chaplin

52 Actress Nazimova

53 Satellite

54 Lendl of tennis

55 Babka, e.g.

57 Detached: Prefix

ACROSS

1 Abrades
6 British cleaning woman
10 Card game
14 His Monday is our Sunday
15 Game divided into chukkers
16 Prong
17 Nocturnal tooters?
19 Keleps
20 Freshen
21 Ophthalmologist's concern
23 Goddess of the rainbow
25 Young hood's neighborhood
26 "I am the __ of Sharon . . ."
29 Deny
32 Fury
35 Actor Sharif
36 Jubilant
37 To be, in Veracruz
38 Parsonage
40 Make into a knight
41 Allen or Frome
43 Song in "A Chorus Line"
44 The highest point
47 Neural network
48 Tuck's companion
49 Most tractable
50 Tax shelters, for short
51 Path for Pompey
53 Russian city

55 Electrical current's strength
59 Stupid
62 What Lear's pobble lacks
63 Some N.F.L. skinheads?
66 Civil wrong
67 Division of a leaf
68 Lines of type
69 Bear on high
70 Zest
71 Concise

DOWN

1 Cheer word
2 Hebrew lyre
3 Beget
4 Baskets
5 Scoff
6 U.S.N. noncom
7 He put ma in stitches
8 Friend in a fray
9 Circular architectural ornament
10 Kind of case or way
11 Royal angler?
12 Flower: Comb. form
13 Dry run
18 Waste away, in Yorkshire
22 Leather that swayed Elvis?
24 Rarely
26 __ candle
27 Native of an Arabian sultanate

28 Gritty flutists?
30 Measurement for a shotgun barrel
31 Under most-favorable conditions
33 Gaucho's rope
34 Piscivorous fliers
39 Gourmand
42 Percussion instrument
45 Allegorical story
46 Practice piece
52 Seed coat

54 Describing some bitterns and flycatchers
55 Aleutian island
56 Fix firmly
57 Jail for Wilde
58 Italian island
60 Vilipend
61 Records of brain elec. activity
64 Kind of mother
65 Reno–to–Las Vegas dir.

SOLUTIONS

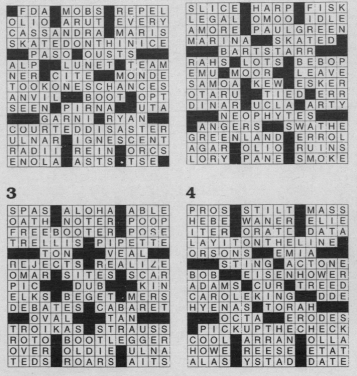

1

	F	D	A		M	O	B	S		R	E	P	E	L
O	L	I	O		A	R	U	T		E	V	E	R	Y
C	A	S	S	A	N	D	R	A		M	A	R	I	S
S	K	A	T	E	D	O	N	T	H	I	N	I	C	E
			P	A	S	O		O	U	S	T	S		
A	L	P			L	U	N	E	T		T	E	A	M
N	E	R		C	I	T	E		M	O	N	D	E	
T	O	O	K	O	N	E	S	C	H	A	N	C	E	S
A	N	V	I	L		B	O	O	T		O	P	T	
S	E	E	N		P	I	R	N	A			U	T	A
		G	A	R	N	I		R	Y	A	N			
C	O	U	R	T	E	D	D	I	S	A	S	T	E	R
U	L	N	A	R		I	G	N	E	S	C	E	N	T
R	A	D	I	I		R	E	I	N		O	R	C	S
E	N	O	L	A		A	S	T	S		T	S	E	

2

S	L	I	C	E		H	A	R	P		F	I	S	K
L	E	G	A	L		O	M	O	O		I	D	L	E
A	M	O	R	E		P	A	U	L	G	R	E	E	N
M	A	R	I	N	A			S	K	A	T	E	D	
		B	A	R	T	S	T	A	R	R				
R	A	H	S		L	O	T	S		B	E	B	O	P
E	M	U		M	O	O	R		L	E	A	V	E	
S	A	M	O	A		K	E	W		E	S	K	E	R
O	T	A	R	U		T	I	E	D		E	R	R	
D	I	N	A	R		U	C	L	A		A	R	T	Y
	N	E	O	P	H	Y	T	E	S					
	A	N	G	E	R	S			S	W	A	T	H	E
G	R	E	E	N	L	A	N	D		E	R	R	O	L
A	G	A	R		O	L	I	O		R	U	I	N	S
L	O	R	Y		P	A	N	E		S	M	O	K	E

3

S	P	A	S		A	L	O	H	A		A	B	L	E
O	A	T	H		N	O	T	E	R		P	O	O	P
F	R	E	E	B	O	O	T	E	R		P	O	S	E
T	R	E	L	L	I	S		P	I	P	E	T	T	E
			T	O	N			V	E	A	L			
R	E	J	E	C	T	S		R	E	A	L	I	Z	E
O	M	A	R		S	I	T	E	S		S	C	A	R
P	I	C			D	U	B			K	I	N		
E	L	K	S		B	E	G	E	T		M	E	R	S
D	E	B	A	T	E	S		C	A	B	A	R	E	T
		O	V	A	L			T	A	N				
T	R	O	I	K	A	S		S	T	R	A	U	S	S
R	O	T	O		B	O	O	T	L	E	G	G	E	R
O	V	E	R		O	L	D	I	E		U	L	N	A
T	E	D	S		R	O	A	R	S		A	I	T	S

4

P	R	O	S		S	T	I	L	T		M	A	S	S
H	E	B	E		W	A	N	E	R		E	L	I	E
I	T	E	R		O	R	A	T	C		D	A	T	A
L	A	Y	I	T	O	N	T	H	E	L	I	N	E	
O	R	S	O	N	S			E	M	I	A			
		S	T	I	N	G		A	C	T	O	N	E	
B	O	B			E	I	S	E	N	H	O	W	E	R
A	D	A	M	S		C	U	R		T	R	E	E	D
C	A	R	O	L	E	K	I	N	G		D	D	E	
H	Y	E	N	A	S		T	O	R	A	H			
		O	C	T	A			E	R	O	D	E	S	
P	I	C	K	U	P	T	H	E	C	H	E	C	K	
C	O	O	L		A	R	R	A	N		O	L	L	A
H	O	W	E		R	E	E	S	E		E	T	A	T
A	L	A	S		Y	S	T	A	D		D	A	T	E

5

L	E	A	S	E		I	T	E	M		L	I	R	A
E	L	T	O	N		L	A	L	A		I	N	A	S
S	M	E	L	T		E	L	I	Z	A	B	E	T	H
T	O	N	E	R	S		C	A	U	S	E	R	I	E
			R	E	A	M	S		M	O	R	T	O	N
M	E	S	S	A	L	A		S	A	N	A			
O	R	T		T	U	R	N	A		E	T	A	T	S
P	A	A	R		S	T	A	N	D		E	R	I	E
E	S	S	E	N		H	A	D	E	S		E	L	A
		G	A	L	A		R	I	T	U	A	L	S	
S	A	L	U	T	E		R	A	C	E	R			
A	B	A	L	A	N	C	E		E	N	A	M	O	R
G	E	R	A	L	D	I	N	E		O	N	I	R	O
A	L	A	R		A	T	T	N		G	I	L	E	S
N	E	S	S		N	Y	S	E		S	A	L	L	Y

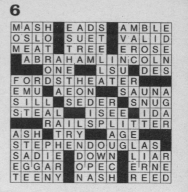

6

M	A	S	H		E	A	D	S		A	M	B	L	E
O	S	L	O		S	U	E	T		V	A	L	I	D
M	E	A	T		T	R	E	E		E	R	O	S	E
	A	B	R	A	H	A	M	L	I	N	C	O	L	N
			O	N	E			L	S	U		D	E	S
F	O	R	D	S	T	H	E	A	T	E	R			
E	M	U		A	E	O	N		S	A	U	N	A	
S	I	L	L		S	E	D	E	R		S	N	U	G
S	T	E	A	L		I	S	E	E			I	D	A
			R	A	I	L	S	P	L	I	T	T	E	R
A	S	H		T	R	Y			A	G	E			
S	T	E	P	H	E	N	D	O	U	G	L	A	S	
S	A	D	I	E		D	O	W	N		L	I	A	R
E	G	G	A	R		O	P	E	C		E	R	N	E
T	E	E	N	Y		N	A	S	H			R	E	E	D

7

S	N	A	P	S		A	L	E	C			S	M	U
T	I	B	I	A		L	A	T	H	S		T	A	G
A	G	E	N	T		A	W	A	I	T		L	I	L
T	H	E	N	U	D	I	S	T	C	O	L	O	N	Y
			A	R	E				H	O	E			
	G	O	L	D	A	N	D	S	I	L	V	E	R	
M	O	I		A	D	O	R	N			E	X	E	S
D	I	L	L	Y		T	O	E		H	E	C	A	N
S	N	E	E		T	O	R	T	A		E	R	Y	
	G	R	A	N	D	O	L	D	E	V	I	L	S	
			R	O	E				L	E	N			
N	O	U	N	T	I	D	Y	C	L	O	T	H	E	S
E	R	R		A	G	R	E	E		N	E	I	G	E
E	G	G		S	N	I	T	S		E	N	T	E	R
D	Y	E		S	P	I	T		S	T	E	R	E	

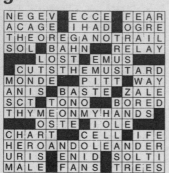

8

S	K	I	S		E	B	S	E	N		P	A	R	A
P	A	R	T		V	A	L	S	E		A	B	A	S
U	N	E	A	S	I	N	E	S	S		L	O	D	I
D	E	S	T	I	N	E	D		T	H	A	L	I	A
			U	N	C		S	O	L	U	T	I	O	N
S	A	V	A	G	E	S		P	I	L	E	S		
A	W	A	R	E		A	R	E	N	A		H	O	W
T	O	N	Y		S	T	I	N	G		D	I	N	E
E	L	D		L	I	E	G	E		S	I	N	C	E
	A	D	E	L	E		D	A	M	A	G	E	D	
E	N	L	I	V	E	N	S		M	I	B			
R	A	I	S	I	N		T	A	I	L	O	R	E	D
N	I	S	H		C	H	A	N	D	E	L	I	E	R
A	L	M	E		E	A	V	E	S		I	G	L	U
S	A	S	S		R	H	E	T	T			C	A	S	T

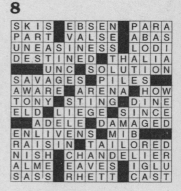

9

N	E	G	E	V		E	C	C	E		F	E	A	R
A	C	A	G	E		I	H	A	D		O	G	R	E
T	H	E	O	R	E	G	A	N	O	T	R	A	I	L
S	O	L		B	A	H	N			R	E	L	A	Y
			L	O	S	T		E	M	U	S			
	C	U	T	S	T	H	E	M	U	S	T	A	R	D
M	O	N	D	E			P	I	T	T		W	A	Y
A	N	I	S		B	A	S	T	E		Z	A	L	E
S	C	T		T	O	N	O			B	O	R	E	D
T	H	Y	M	E	O	N	M	Y	H	A	N	D	S	
			O	S	T	E		I	O	L	E			
C	H	A	R	T			C	E	L	L		I	F	E
H	E	R	O	A	N	D	O	L	E	A	N	D	E	R
U	R	I	S		E	N	I	D		S	O	L	T	I
M	A	L	E		F	A	N	S		T	R	E	E	S

10

C	A	R	P	S		C	A	W			T	R	A	P
O	L	E	A	N		A	G	A			H	O	R	A
D	A	N	T	E		P	O	L	I	C	E	M	A	N
E	S	T	R	E	A	T		E	N	A	M	E	L	S
			O	R	L	O	P		C	S	A			
E	T	A	L		A	R	O	M	A	S		A	U	K
F	B	I	M	A	N		R	E	S	A	D	D	L	E
L	A	M	A	S		S	T	A		V	E	I	N	E
A	R	E	N	S	K	Y	S		B	A	T	M	A	N
T	S	E		A	E	R	O	B	E		E	E	E	S
			S	U	I		F	R	A	N	C			
I	N	S	U	L	T	O		I	M	I	T	A	T	E
C	O	N	S	T	A	B	L	E		V	I	B	E	S
A	M	O	I		O	A	F		E	V	E	N	T	
N	E	B	E		E	D	S		N	E	S	T	S	

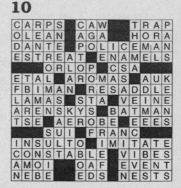

204

11

```
S H A D   T E S L A   C A L F
E I R E   O G E E S   O L I O
A L M S   E A R T H Q U A K E
L O A T H I N G   C U R S E S
    G R I N   E C L A T
  G E O R G E   H O I S T E D
R E D Y E   C L A U S   I L E
A N D S   C H O R D   I D O L
F R O   R O O S T   A M A P A
T E N S I L E   S A M P L E
    T S A R S   B O O B
A C U M E N   T R A I T O R S
S A N A N D R E A S   E R I E
S T I R   E E R I E   N E N E
N O S Y   R E N D S   T S K S
```

12

```
B A N G   S L A G   S P E E D
E L O I   H O L A   E A T M E
S O D A   R O O T   G R A M A
S W I N G I N G O N A S T A R
    W A V Y   R O L E
D E F I L E   A B T   E M I L
A L O N E   A M O I   A L E
F L Y I N G D O W N T O R I O
F I L   I D O L   E V I A N
Y S E R   V I N   S P E N D A
    A B E T   A P E R
S I N G I N I N T H E R A I N
I D I O T   V O T E   U P T O
M I N U S   E M A R   L E T O
P E A T Y   S E R E   E X O N
```

13

```
A O R T A   A N N E   U N I T
B R O W N   B U O Y   L O N E
C A B O T L O D G E   T O G A
S D S   H I D E   T U R N E R
    W O V E   F O R A
S T A I N   B L O O M E R S
T R U L Y   T O U T   O M I T
A A B B   T R U T H   D E N E
G L E E   E I R E   D E N S E
G A R R I S O N   O R D E R
    F A T S   S H U N
R A M O N A   S I E G   N S W
O D O R   T E S S E L L A T E
D I S C   O T T S   A S T E R
E T T E   R O S Y   S T O W E
```

14

```
  S A G O S   S P A   F O R D
L E V A N T   D O R   A R E A
B R E W E R   A P O P L E X Y
J A C K N I C K L A U S
    S O D A   A R R E A R S
C B S   E N G R   S T R O M
H O O   I N N O   U T I L E
A U G U S T A N A T I O N A L
F R O N T   G I R T   O N T
E N O C H   I S L E   S D S
R E D L E G S   E S T E
  A R N O L D P A L M E R
P H A S E O U T   A S T E R O
E A R P   M R G   S T O L I D
A L M S   E S S   S E N D S
```

15

```
O R C A   R O B I N   S C A N
N E A P   A D E L E   T I L E
C A M P A N E L L A   E N D O
E M E R G E N T   T O L D O N
    A R E S   C H I L E
L U C I E   E A R   L A R E S
A R I S E N   T O N Y   E V A
M I T E   E L O P E   G L I B
I E R   P E A N   A P O L L O
A L O N E   L E M   R O A S T
    N O R M A   U S E D
A C E D I A   T R E E N A I L
C O L D   D A R D A N E L L A
I L L E   A B E E T   S I K H
D E A D   M E T R O   S T A R
```

16

```
  S G T   S S T   S U M A C
S A L E   P E E R   P L A Y A
A T O R   O M N I   L A R R Y
L I B E R T I N E   A N T S
I R A T E   N E S T Y   I H S
C E L E B R A T O R   A N I L
      O E R   N O W H E R E
A S S E R T     W A S T E D
D E M O N I C   N E F
A M O N   R O Y A L F L U S H
M I L   M E N E N   L A N C E
  P L E A   C O N G E S T E D
A R E N T   A M I E   C O N G
L O T T E   V E E R   A L E E
A S T O R   E N S   R D S
```

17

```
BOAS .ABEAM.VALE
LIRE.CULPA.EMIL
ALEXANDERS.ROLL
SETTLE.VICTORIA
TREED..ELOIN...
..TAPIN.TRICOT.
OAT.LOS..ECOLE.
CLEMSON.RESALES
.ASCAP..SAG.TOT
.SOHRAB.ANGER..
...ISLET.RESET.
ROSEMARY.FIANCE
ABET.MARGUERITE
FORT.ETIAM.EDAM
FETA.SOCLE.DELS
```

18

```
BILL.EMMA.APART
EDIE.MOAB.DIXIE
TORN.URNS.VOICE
ELATE.DICKINSON
...IRMA.EASE...
GILLIAN.STEEDS.
ONE.CAT.SERRIED
ALIP.....SAGE..
DEGRADE.MOA.NAE
.THELAP.INFIELD
...ALBI.STAB...
WORCESTER.RIVER
OMAHA.ONUS.DEMI
ROVER.MILO.ERIN
DOERS.EDEN.MARK
```

19

```
OAST.LOCUS..PATE
BRIE.INANE.AMOS
ENGLISHMEN.PAYS
YEN.FLIP..CANOE
...THEMIDDAYSUN
ADORES..ARIA...
CORE..SANER.FED
TOBEAMISSIONARY
ARS.TENSE..OUSE
...ALEC.EVENED.
PRIVATELIVES...
RUNES..INIT.TEA
ODOR.NOELCOWARD
VENT.BEGAT.ATLI
ORES.CREWS.DIET
```

20

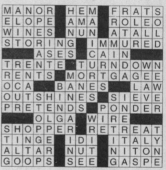

```
MANOR.HEM.FRATS
ELOPE.AMA.ROLEO
WINES.NUN.ATALL
STORING.IMMURED
....ASES.CAIN..
TRENTE.TURNDOWN
RENTS.MORTGAGEE
OCA.BANES..LAW.
OUTSHINES.SIEVE
PRETENDS.PONDER
..OLGA.WIRE....
SHOPPER.RETREAT
TINGE.IDI.ITALY
ALTAR.NUT.NITON
GOOPS.SEE.GASPE
```

21

```
CHILI.OAFS.MASH
LORAN.SLAM.ELLE
APART.SITE.SCOW
ROTE...CLASHES
ONEDAYATATIME..
.OMELET..LAMBS
ASP.BAIT..TIRE
TWOFORTHESEESAW
TALA..ELAL.TDS
UNITE.GRETAS...
.THREESCOMPANY
ALBERTA..EDIE
DOUR.URGE.OCALA
ACRE.DEAN.FINES
MOOD.EDGE.FEAST
```

22

```
GAPS.HAHA..PLAY
IGOT.EXIT.WHERE
GAGA.MITE.HOSEA
IRONFIST.TINEAR
...DON.INONE...
ATLAS.STORE.SSR
LAIRS.TESS..THE
GLADEYE.HOTHEAD
AER.ORAE.RANDY
ESS.SUERS.ANOSE
...PINOT.ESD...
PEGLEG.HIGHBROW
ADIEU.DUCE.AIDE
CEDAR.EROS.GLIB
ENES.ISNT.SECS
```

23

S	T	A	I	R	S			S	P	A	R	E	D
P	A	N	N	I	E	R		P	L	A	T	E	A	U
E	N	N	O	B	L	E		E	A	S	T	E	R	N
A	G	O	N		F	E	L	O	N	S		L	I	D
R	O	Y		L	I	N	T		D	I	N	E
S	E	E	M		L	E	N	S		R	A	N	G	E
	D	R	Y	D	O	C	K		H	A	N	G	S
		O	U	S	T		P	A	N	G
	R	U	P	E	E		T	O	L	T	E	C	S
R	E	M	I	T		M	O	R	E		R	O	T	I
E	L	B	A		B	A	L	T		R	U	N
G	A	R		P	R	I	D	E	S		R	O	D	S
I	T	A	L	I	A	N		N	O	M	I	N	E	E
N	E	G	A	T	E	S		T	R	I	D	E	N	T
A	D	E	P	T	S			E	X	E	R	T	S

24

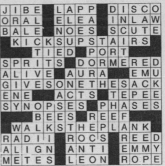

J	I	B	E		L	A	P	P		D	I	S	C	O
O	R	A	L		E	L	E	A		I	N	L	A	W
B	A	L	E		N	O	E	S		S	C	U	T	E
	K	I	C	K	S	U	P	S	T	A	I	R	S
			T	I	E	D		P	O	R	T
S	P	R	I	T	S		D	O	R	M	E	R	E	D
A	L	I	V	E		A	U	R	A		E	M	U
G	I	V	E	S	O	N	E	T	H	E	S	A	C	K
E	N	E		A	C	T	S		T	E	P	E	E
S	Y	N	O	P	S	E	S		P	H	A	S	E	S
		B	E	E	S		R	E	E	F
W	A	L	K	S	T	H	E	P	L	A	N	K
R	A	D	I	I		R	O	C	S		R	E	E	D
A	L	I	G	N		A	N	T	I		E	M	M	Y
M	E	T	E	S		L	E	O	N		R	O	P	E

25

S	T	S		P	A	R	O	S		U	P	P	E	R
O	R	O		A	P	O	R	T		T	O	O	L	E
N	O	R	T	H	P	O	L	E		E	L	L	E	R
N	I	T	A		A	M	O	R	E	S		E	V	A
E	K	E	R		L	I	N	E	T		A	M	A	T
T	A	D	P	O	L	E		S	P	R	I	T	E
			U	S	S	R		O	O	Z	E	D
A	P	E	S		T	I	R		E	W	E	S
S	N	O	R	T		B	E	S	S
A	T	L	A	S	T		M	A	Y	P	O	L	E
P	E	E	L		A	S	P	I	C		O	T	I	S
I	N	C		S	W	A	R	T	H		M	I	S	T
E	N	A	T	E		T	O	T	E	M	P	O	L	E
N	A	T	E	S		O	V	E	T	A		S	E	R
T	E	S	T	S		N	O	R	S	E		E	S	S

26

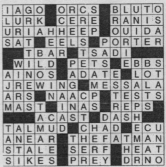

I	A	G	O		O	R	C	S		B	L	U	T	O
L	U	R	K		C	E	R	E		R	A	N	I	S
U	R	I	A	H	H	E	E	P		O	U	I	D	A
S	A	T		E	E	L	S		P	O	R	T	E	R
		T	B	A	R		T	S	A	D	I
	W	I	L	D		P	E	T	S		E	B	B	S
A	I	N	O	S		A	D	A	T	E		L	O	T
J	R	E	W	I	N	G		M	E	S	S	A	L	A
A	R	S		N	A	A	C	P		T	E	S	T	S
M	A	S	T		I	N	A	S		R	E	P	S
		A	C	A	S	T		D	A	S	H
T	A	L	M	U	D		C	H	A	D		E	C	U
A	N	E	A	R		T	H	E	F	A	T	M	A	N
S	T	A	L	E		S	E	R	F		H	E	A	T
S	I	K	E	S		P	R	E	Y		D	R	N	O

27

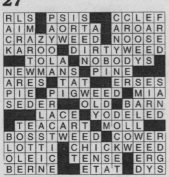

R	L	S		P	S	I	S		C	C	L	E	F
A	I	M		A	O	R	T	A		A	R	O	A	R
C	R	A	Z	Y	W	E	E	D		N	O	O	S	E
K	A	R	O	O		D	I	R	T	Y	W	E	E	D
		T	O	L	A		N	O	B	O	D	Y	S
N	E	W	M	A	N	S		P	I	N	E
A	R	E	S		T	A	T		E	R	S	E	S
P	I	E		P	I	G	W	E	E	D		M	I	A
S	E	D	E	R		O	L	D		B	A	R	N
	L	A	C	E		Y	O	D	E	L	E	D
T	E	A	C	A	R	T		M	O	L	L
B	O	S	S	T	W	E	E	D		C	O	W	E	R
L	O	T	T	I		C	H	I	C	K	W	E	E	D
O	L	E	I	C		T	E	N	S	E		E	R	G
B	E	R	N	E		E	T	A	T		D	Y	S

28

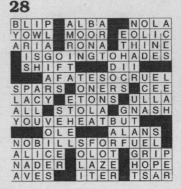

B	L	I	P		A	L	B	A		N	O	L	A
Y	O	W	L		M	O	O	R		E	O	L	I	C
A	R	I	A		R	O	N	A		T	H	I	N	E
	I	S	G	O	I	N	G	T	O	H	A	D	E	S
	S	H	I	F	T			D	I	I
		A	F	A	T	E	S	O	C	R	U	E	L
S	P	A	R	S		O	N	E	R	S		C	E	E
L	A	C	Y		E	T	O	N	S		U	L	L	A
A	L	L		S	T	O	L	A		G	N	A	S	H
Y	O	U	V	E	H	E	A	T	B	U	T
		O	L	E			A	L	A	N	S
N	O	B	I	L	L	S	F	O	R	F	U	E	L
A	L	I	C	E		O	L	O	T		G	R	I	P
N	A	D	E	R		L	A	Z	E		H	O	P	E
A	V	E	S		I	T	E	R		T	S	A	R

29

```
M A L T A   D I P   P O O R
A L I E N   S A R I   I M R E
S T A N G   O V A L   C A D S
H O R S E T H I E F   K N E E
      L E O N   E M P I R E
P R I S O N   C U R I O
A H O T   E R I C   S C A M
D E L I C T I   L O C K S U P
  E A C H   S P A N   E T S I
    K O R E A   E S T A T E
S E D U C E   T E A K
T R I P   B U R G L A R I E S
R O O M   A R O A   T O R S O
E D D A   T A L L   E L A N D
P E E N   E L S   R E N E S
```

30

```
B O M B   T E R R A   M A D
A V E R   S T E E R   D A R E
N A M E   P H A S E   E L L A
G L O A T   E D U C A T I O N
    T H O R   L A L A
I S T H E B E S T   T I A R A
N E A   N E A T   D O L L A R
F I S H   S L A V E   S I T S
E N T I R E   R I L L   B I O
R E E S E   P R O V I S I O N
    T E A L   L E F T
F O R O L D A G E   E I G E R
I G O R   A N E N T   N A V E
S L A Y   P E N C E   G L E N
T E N   T R E E D   Y A R D
```

31

```
E R S T   R O O M S   C O M B
B O A R   E C L A T   A P I E
B O R A   P E D R O   R E N T
  F I V E E A S Y P I E C E S
    E L A N   P O E
  A V R I L   B I A N N U A L
E G E S T   P A N G   P E I
T H R E E M U S K E T E E R S
R A S   E L I S   O M N I A
E S O T E R I C   S T A D E
  O T C   W A A C
T H E F O U R M I L L I O N
H A L F   R A I T T   A P O D
A L O E   I N T H E   T A R E
N O N E   C I T E D   E L M O
```

32

```
A M A   A D A N A   S H I P
L I L I   S O L E D   T O G O
P L A N E T O F T H E A P E S
  D I S A R M S   E N M I T Y
    I T A   R T E
D O G D A Y A F T E R N O O N
E R L E   G O O S E   L A E
P A I S A   A S S   E L I T E
O C D   R A I S E   A W E D
T H E B A D N E W S B E A R S
    O R A   P A R
B A L S A M   T R E E T O P
I C E S T A T I O N Z E B R A
E R N E   N I T I D   S O O N
R E A D   T O O L S   E F T
```

33

```
S T O P   T A R E S   D U M P
L U L U   O M U T A   A T E E
O L D B L O O D A N D G U T S
G E E   A L E E   E G R E T
    S C O B   A S C E N D S
H A P P Y W A R R I O R
E R I E   O M A R   L A B
R E N D   S P A S M   L O L A
O A T   G E L S   I T A L
  G R E A T H O U D I N I
I M P L A N T   A L S O
S A L A D   O N D E   A K A
T H E R E F R I G E R A T O R
L A B E   O A S E S   G O B I
E N E S   I N E R T   A P E D
```

34

```
M O C H A   S P A R   H A R M
E L L E R   H E R O   O H I O
A L A R M   O R A L   K E A S
N A M B Y P A M B Y   E A T S
    M E T   P A Y D A Y
R A G T A G   C L O M P
A L L I N   G O A L P O S T S
L E E R   P A N S Y   K E E L
E X E R C I S E S   C E L L A
    A R C H Y   W A Y L A Y
M U K L U K   E R R
A B R I   W I L L Y N I L L Y
R O A R   I R A S   A L I A S
L A I R   C A D I   G E S T E
A T T A   K N E E   E S T E R
```

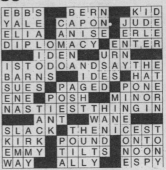

35

H	E	R	A		B	I	T	S		B	A	S	T
B	E	R	E	T		I	D	E	A		R	U	H	R
A	B	O	V	E	B	O	A	R	D		O	T	O	E
R	E	S	O	L	U	T	E		D	E	M	O	N	S
			L	I	R	A		B	E	T	I	M	E	S
E	L	A	T	E	S		D	O	R	A	D	O		
I	O	U		R	A	T	E	R		L	I	T	H	E
R	O	T	C		R	O	P	E	D		C	I	O	N
E	T	H	A	N		A	T	R	E	E		V	E	T
	O	R	E	A	D	S		T	A	T	E	R	S	
C	A	R	P	E	L	S		A	E	R	O			
A	B	S	O	R	B		A	B	S	T	R	U	S	E
B	O	H	R		A	N	T	I	T	H	E	S	I	S
E	D	I	T		N	O	T	E		E	R	E	D	E
R	E	P	S		S	A	N	S		N	O	D	E	

36

E	B	B	S		B	E	R	N			K	I	D
Y	A	L	E		C	A	P	O	N		J	U	D	E
E	L	I	A		A	N	I	S	E		E	R	L	E
D	I	P	L	O	M	A	C	Y		E	N	T	E	R
			I	D	E	N		U	R	N				
I	S	T	O	D	O	A	N	D	S	A	Y	T	H	E
B	A	R	N	S			I	D	E	S		H	A	T
S	U	E	S		P	A	G	E	D		P	O	N	E
E	N	E		P	O	S	H			M	I	N	O	R
N	A	S	T	I	E	S	T	T	H	I	N	G	I	N
			A	N	T			W	A	N	E			
S	L	A	C	K		T	H	E	N	I	C	E	S	T
K	I	R	K		P	O	U	N	D		O	N	T	O
E	M	M	Y		T	I	L	T	S		N	O	O	N
W	A	Y		A	L	L	Y			E	S	P	Y	

37

M	A	S	S		S	W	A	L	E		S	E	W	S
E	S	N	E		A	I	R	E	S		A	W	R	Y
T	H	E	C	O	N	S	T	I	T	U	T	I	O	N
E	Y	E		D	I	P	S			S	A	N	T	O
			N	E	T	S		F	L	A	N	G	E	D
T	H	E	O	R	Y		L	I	E	N	S			
E	A	V	E		S	E	R	A	C		R	I	O	
T	H	E	L	A	W	O	F	T	H	E	L	A	N	D
E	S	S		N	O	R	T	H		A	N	T	I	
	S	T	O	R	Y		C	O	T	T	O	N		
T	O	T	A	L	L	Y		C	A	P	E			
E	C	O	L	E		D	A	R	E		A	W	E	
A	T	T	O	R	N	E	Y	G	E	N	E	R	A	L
K	E	E	N		E	R	N	E	S		L	I	I	I	I
S	T	R	S		W	E	E	D	S		M	A	T	S

38

J	I	N	N	I		D	O	B	B	Y		P	A	N
A	R	I	E	L		O	L	L	A	E		E	K	E
P	O	L	T	E	R	G	E	I	S	T		R	I	A
	N	E	O		Y	E	A	S	T		G	I	M	P
			P	P	D			S	E	G	O			
E	L	F		H	E	S	S		D	Y	B	B	U	K
M	A	L	F	O	R	M	E	D		P	L	E	I	N
O	R	I	O	N		E	A	R		S	I	G	N	E
T	E	R	R	A		E	L	I	M	I	N	A	T	E
E	S	T	A	T	E		S	P	E	E		T	A	D
			G	E	M	S		D	S	C				
W	I	N	E		M	O	T	T	O		R	A	E	
A	M	E		L	E	P	R	E	C	H	A	U	N	S
S	P	A		E	T	H	E	R		A	T	R	I	A
H	S	T		E	S	S	E	N		M	E	A	D	E

39

E	R	N	E	S	T			S	A	B	R	I	N	A
L	O	O	N	I	E	R		T	I	R	E	M	E	N
A	D	V	E	R	S	E		A	R	A	L	S	E	A
T	E	E		S	T	A	B	L	E		A	O	R	T
H	O	L	Y			C	R	E	D	I	T			
			E	A	S	T	E	R		M	E	T	A	L
T	H	E	S	W	E	E	T		S	P	R	U	C	E
O	A	R		H	A	D		S	P	A		R	I	G
R	U	S	H	I	N		A	M	E	R	I	N	D	S
S	T	E	E	L		S	L	E	E	T	S			
			R	E	P	E	A	L		O	B	O	E	
M	E	D	E		A	V	I	L	A	S		E	P	I
I	M	I	T	A	T	E		O	R	A	N	G	E	S
R	E	S	I	D	E	R		F	I	X	T	U	R	E
S	U	C	C	E	S	S			L	E	H	M	A	N

40

S	A	G		B	A	Y	E	D		C	U	B	E
A	M	O	K		E	V	O	K	E		O	P	A	L
B	Y	A	N	D	L	A	R	G	E		A	T	R	I
A	S	T	E	R	I	S	K		P	A	S	H	A	S
			A	I	N	T		R	E	N	T	E		
E	R	O	D	E	D		C	O	N	N	E	C	T	S
Y	E	N		S	A	L	A	S		E	R	R	O	L
O	C	T	S		S	O	N	I	N		S	E	R	A
T	A	H	O	E		T	O	N	E	S		E	R	I
S	P	E	C	T	A	T	E		A	W	A	K	E	N
			B	R	A	S	S		D	R	E	I		
S	P	L	A	T	S		T	R	E	A	T	I	S	E
A	L	I	T		I	N	S	E	A	R	C	H	O	F
G	E	N	E		C	R	A	G	S		H	A	L	T
O	A	K	S		K	A	R	S	T		D	O	S	

41

F	L	E	A	S		N	A	N	A		S	T	A	S
L	O	A	T	H		O	L	E	G		H	O	W	E
A	T	S	E	A		N	A	V	A	J	O	J	O	E
P	I	T	A	P	A	T		A	M	A	P	O	L	A
			S	E	C	O	N	D	A	C	T			
V	A	S	E		I	X	I	A		K	A	P	P	A
E	S	T		E	D	I	T		P	L	E	A	D	
S	T	E	R	N		C	R	O		O	K	A	P	I
P	I	L	A	F		A	B	E	T		L	A	O	
A	N	E	M	O		S	T	E	M		S	E	W	S
		P	R	O	C	E	D	U	R	E				
T	R	E	A	C	L	E		I	S	A	D	O	R	A
V	E	N	G	E	A	N	C	E		G	A	M	A	L
E	D	I	E		F	I	N	N		E	T	A	P	E
R	O	D	S		S	C	O	T		D	E	N	S	E

42

F	I	J	I		D	O	N	A	R		C	O	R	A
A	D	A	R		E	P	O	D	E		O	M	E	N
M	O	C	K		M	A	R	I	A		R	A	N	T
E	L	K		J	O	H	N	M	C	E	N	R	O	E
		K	N	O	T			T	S	E				
M	A	R	I	N	E		T	R	I	S	T	A	N	S
O	R	A	L	S		L	E	A	V	E		R	E	T
D	E	M	E		K	A	T	I	E		I	T	M	O
E	N	E		D	I	N	E	D		P	S	H	A	W
S	A	R	D	I	N	E	S		S	A	L	U	T	E
		R	A	G				I	C	E	R			
D	O	N	A	L	D	B	U	D	G	E		A	P	T
A	L	O	G		O	R	L	O	N		A	S	E	A
W	I	N	O		M	A	N	T	A		S	H	A	M
S	O	O	N		S	T	A	E	L		P	E	R	E

43

I	M	A	M		E	R	E	C	T		S	T	A	R
M	O	N	A		D	E	A	R	E		H	E	R	O
P	A	N	J	A	N	D	R	U	M		E	E	R	O
A	N	E		C	A	D		P	L	A	T	E	N	
L	E	A	P	T		E	E	R	I	E		O	S	E
A	D	L	A	I		R	A	H		N	A	T	T	Y
		L	O	A		R	E	O		M	U	S	S	
		C	A	N	D	E	L	A	B	R	U	M		
	D	I	E	T		A	L	I		E	E	L		
E	A	R	E	D		L	E	A		P	E	S	C	E
A	C	E		Y	E	A	R	N		E	T	H	A	N
R	O	B	L	E	S		G	O	A		A	N	A	
E	C	R	U		T	W	E	E	D	L	E	D	U	M
S	C	U	T		O	P	E	R	A		V	E	T	O
T	A	M	E		P	A	N	S	Y		E	D	E	R

44

D	E	L	T	A		D	I	M		E	T	A	G	E
A	M	I	E	S		E	S	E		L	U	B	E	S
D	U	T	C	H	S	E	T	T	L	E	M	E	N	T
		H	E	L	P	S		A	M	B	L	E		
	T	E	N	S	E				N	I	L			
T	O	D	O		E	R	A	S	E		E	D	D	A
A	L	I		S	T	A	R	T		P	R	E	E	N
P	E	T	E	R	S	T	U	Y	V	E	S	A	N	T
I	D	E	A	S		E	L	L	A	S		L	I	E
R	O	D	S		T	R	E	E	S		T	E	E	S
			T	R	I				A	V	E	R	S	
		B	E	L	I	E		A	C	R	E	S		
N	E	W	Y	O	R	K	S	H	I	S	T	O	R	Y
A	M	E	N	T		E	T	A		T	E	P	E	E
B	A	R	N	S		N	A	P		A	D	A	P	T

45

M	A	L	T		E	S	T	E	S		O	M	N	I
A	T	E	E		T	E	A	R	Y		N	E	O	N
S	T	A	N	T	H	E	M	A	N		C	A	L	K
S	U	N	S	H	A	D	E		O	R	A	L	L	Y
			C	A	N	E		A	D	U	L	T		
A	R	S	O	N		D	A	M		S	L	I	C	K
T	O	U	R	E	D		R	O	S	E		C	H	I
L	U	P	E		A	W	O	K	E		S	K	I	N
A	T	E		S	K	I	M		A	R	L	E	N	E
S	E	R	G	E		S	A	C		O	U	T	E	R
		C	R	E	P	E		A	R	U	G			
A	T	H	E	N	A		D	R	U	G	G	I	S	T
C	H	I	T		T	H	E	M	A	H	A	T	M	A
T	E	E	N		H	O	L	E	D		R	O	O	K
S	O	F	A		S	P	I	N	E		D	O	G	E

46

T	A	C	O		F	L	E	A		E	L	U	D	E
O	B	O	L		L	O	S	T		C	A	N	U	S
H	E	A	D	F	O	R	T	H	E	H	I	L	L	S
A	L	T	E	R	E	D		O	V	O		A	L	E
V	E	E	R	Y		M	M	E		S	W	A	N	
E	S	S		P	L	I	E		A	L	F	R	E	
			G	I	L	E	S		C	L	O	U	D	S
	H	E	A	D	O	V	E	R	H	E	E	L	S	
H	E	M	M	E	D		R	O	U	E	S			
A	R	B	U	S		C	L	O	G		M	O	M	
L	I	A	T		R	O	Y		A	R	O	M	A	
S	T	R		I	E	R		R	E	C	E	D	E	S
T	A	K	E	T	O	O	N	E	S	H	E	E	L	S
O	G	E	E	S		N	I	N	A		K	L	E	E
N	E	D	R	A		A	B	O	U		S	S	T	S

47

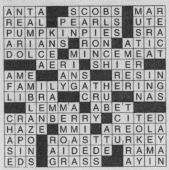

A	N	T	A			S	C	O	B	S		M	A	R
R	E	A	L		P	E	A	R	L	S		U	T	E
P	U	M	P	K	I	N	P	I	E	S		S	R	A
A	R	I	A	N	S		R	O	N		A	T	I	C
D	O	L	C	E		M	I	N	C	E	M	E	A	T
		A	E	R	I			S	H	I	E	R		
A	M	E		A	N	S			R	E	S	I	N	
F	A	M	I	L	Y	G	A	T	H	E	R	I	N	G
L	I	B	R	A		C	R	U		N	A	S		
	L	E	M	M	A		A	B	E	T				
C	R	A	N	B	E	R	R	Y		C	I	T	E	D
H	A	Z	E		M	M	I		A	R	E	O	L	A
A	P	O		R	O	A	S	T	T	U	R	K	E	Y
S	I	N		A	I	D	E	D	E		R	A	M	A
E	D	S		G	R	A	S	S		A	Y	I	N	

48

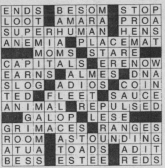

E	N	D	S		B	E	S	O	M		S	T	O	P
L	O	O	T		A	M	A	R	A		P	R	O	A
S	U	P	E	R	H	U	M	A	N		H	E	N	S
A	N	E	M	I	A		P	L	A	C	E	M	A	T
			M	O	M	S		S	T	A	R	E		
C	A	P	I	T	A	L	S		E	R	E	N	O	W
E	A	R	N	S		A	L	M	E	S		D	N	A
S	L	O	G		A	D	I	O	S		C	O	I	N
T	E	D		F	L	E	E	T		S	A	U	C	E
A	N	I	M	A	L		R	E	P	U	L	S	E	D
		G	A	L	O	P		L	E	S	E			
G	R	I	M	A	C	E	S		R	A	N	G	E	S
R	O	O	M		A	S	T	O	U	N	D	I	N	G
A	T	U	A		T	O	A	D	S		A	D	I	T
B	E	S	S		E	S	T	E	E		R	E	D	S

49

D	A	U	B	S		T	O	M	B		I	M	A	M
A	G	L	E	T		W	W	I	I		M	E	D	E
H	O	U	S	E	C	A	L	L	S		A	D	A	R
			T	R	O	Y		L	E	S	S	I	N	G
B	O	W	I	N	G		P	E	C	K		C	O	E
O	V	E	R		E	M	U		T	I	T	I		
P	O	L		K	N	E	E	L		R	I	N	G	
S	I	L	E	N	T	T	R	E	A	T	M	E	N	T
	D	A	D	O		S	I	N	U	S		H	O	E
	N	O	L	O		L	O	G		G	A	M	E	
S	A	D		L	U	T	E		E	M	O	T	E	D
A	U	G	U	S	T	A		E	R	A	S			
O	D	O	R		W	H	A	T	S	U	P	D	O	C
N	E	O	N		I	O	N	A		D	E	A	N	E
E	N	D	S		T	E	N	T		E	L	W	A	Y

50

P	I	A	F		R	A	B	B	I		P	A	S	T
A	T	T	U		E	R	I	E	S		L	M	N	O
N	E	O	N		F	U	N	N	Y	P	A	P	E	R
G	R	I	N	D	I	N	G		O	U	T	L	E	T
			Y	E	N		S	H	U	N	T	E	R	S
C	R	A	B	B	E	R		A	R	S				
L	O	G	O		R	A	N	T			F	A	I	T
A	M	E	N		S	T	E	E	D		U	P	T	O
M	E	D	E			T	O	R	E		N	O	O	N
			A	S	E		S	P	I	N	D	L	F	
S	A	D	D	L	E	R	S		L	A	Y			
A	R	E	O	L	E		E	L	O	N	G	A	T	E
F	U	N	N	Y	M	O	N	E	Y		I	R	I	S
E	L	S	A		E	R	O	S	E		R	E	N	T
S	E	E	R		D	A	R	E	D		L	O	G	E

51

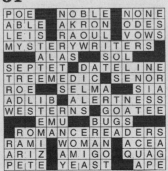

P	O	E		N	O	B	L	E		N	O	N	E	
A	B	L	E		A	K	R	O	N		O	D	E	S
L	E	I	S		R	A	O	U	L		V	O	W	S
M	Y	S	T	E	R	Y	W	R	I	T	E	R	S	
			A	L	A	S			S	O	L			
S	E	P	T	E	T		D	A	T	E	L	I	N	E
T	R	E	E	M	E	D	I	C		S	E	N	O	R
R	O	E		S	E	L	M	A			S	I	A	
A	D	L	I	B		A	L	E	R	T	N	E	S	S
W	E	S	T	E	R	N	S		G	O	A	T	E	E
			E	M	U		B	U	G	S				
R	O	M	A	N	C	E	R	E	A	D	E	R	S	
R	A	M	I		W	O	M	A	N		A	C	E	A
A	R	I	Z		A	M	I	G	O		Q	U	A	G
P	E	T	E		Y	E	A	S	T		A	P	E	

52

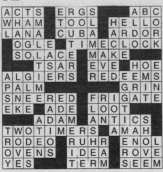

A	C	T	S		E	R	G	S			A	B	C	
W	H	A	M		T	O	O	L		H	E	L	L	O
L	A	N	A		C	U	B	A		A	R	D	O	R
O	G	L	E		T	I	M	E	C	L	O	C	K	
S	O	L	A	C	E		M	A	K	E				
	T	S	A	R		E	V	E		H	O	E		
A	L	G	I	E	R	S		R	E	D	E	E	M	S
P	A	L	M							G	R	I	N	
S	N	E	E	R	E	D		F	R	I	G	A	T	E
E	K	E		A	D	E		L	O	O	T			
	A	D	A	M		A	N	T	I	C	S			
T	W	O	T	I	M	E	R	S		A	M	A	H	
R	O	D	E	O		R	U	H	R		E	N	O	L
O	V	E	N	S		I	D	E	A		R	O	V	E
Y	E	S		T	E	R	M		S	E	E	M		

211

53

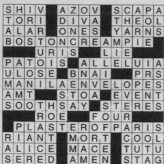

```
S H I V   A Z O V   S C A P A
T O R I   D I V A   T H E O L
A L A R   O N E S   Y A R N S
B O S T O N C R E A M P I E
      U R I S     L I E
P A T O I S   A L L E L U I A
U L O S E   B N A I   P R S
M A N I L A E N V E L O P E S
A M T   S T O A   E V E N T
S O O T H S A Y   S T E R E S
    R O E     F O U R
  P L A S T E R O F P A R I S
R I A N T   M O R T   C O O L
A L I C E   M A C E   T U T U
S E R E D   A M E N   S T A G
```

54

```
B A L A S   J I L T   P A M S
L E A D A   E S A U   I D Y L
O R N O T   R E I N   E Z R A
N I T P I C K E R   I B E A M
D E S T R Y     R N A
    E E R O   N E G L I G E
W O O D S   S C A L E D O W N
E O N   P A L S Y   W E D
F L Y W E I G H T   W E A N S
T A X A B L E   S P I N
    S R I     A R G A L I
H A R P O   M O T H E A T E N
E Q U I   L E V I   T R I A L
R U S S   E R I K   A D O R A
B A T H   O L D E   P E N N Y
```

55

```
A L D A   C A S A   A W F U L
R E U P   A M P S   V E R N E
I T E R   N Y E T   A R E A S
E M P I R E   E R S   E E L S
L E R O I   E D O U A R D
  O R N E R Y   C R E O L E
H A C I E N D A   A D M E N
A L E   D E N S E   O A T
T E S L A   D I S T A F F S
S E S A M E   P R E E N S
  O M I N O U S   C O P S E
S O F A   S U B   O S T E E N
E G L I N   S L A V   H E R S
E R A S E   T I G E   E C R U
N E W T S   S C A R   R H E E
```

56

```
C A R D   S A N S   O B A D
O M O O   C R A M   P L A T O
M O O N S H I N E   H E L O T
A S T U T E   C A B O O D L E
    T O M M Y R O T   E L D
A L F   W E E   B O A R
M E L E E   L I M B   N D A K
O V A L   H O O E Y   T A R N
R I P S   A N N E   D I S C O
    D E A D   S C I   H A W
A D O   F A L D E R A L
P R O M O T E R   A R O M A S
R O D E O   P O P P Y C O C K
I N L E T   T O R E   K I N E
L E E K   A P O D   S L E W
```

57

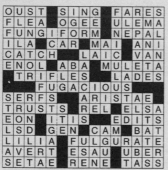

```
O U S T   S I N G   F A R E S
F L E A   O G E E   U L E M A
F U N G I F O R M   N E P A L
I L A   C A R   M A I   A N I
C A T C H   L A I C   V A N
E N O L   A B A   M U L E T A
  T R I F L E S   L A D E S
      F U G A C I O U S
S E R F S   A R I S T A E
T R U S T S   R E L   E L S A
E O N   I T I S   E D I T S
L S D   G E N   C A M   B A T
L I L I A   F U L G U R A T E
A V E R T   E S A U   U B E R
S E T A E   R E N E   T A S S
```

58

```
  D E F A M E S   L O B O S
S O L E C I S M   T R A D E R
I N I T I A T E   S T R O D E
E N D E D   A L L   S E M I S
V E E S   A T T A R   D E M E
E R S   C R E S T E D   T E N
    E A T S   E V I D E N T
C O N S U L     E X E R T S
A M A S S E S   P R E Y
R E P   E S C O R T S   M A P
A L O P   S A V E S   C A L L
C E L L I   R E M   C A R T A
A T E A S E   R I P A R I A N
S T O N E R   D E E R P A R K
  E N T R E   O R D A I N S
```

59

```
BIBB AMOLE COLT
ANOA SATED ALOE
ANYHOWTHEHOLEIN
SSS PETER BLOND
  BALER  ULE
BEFALLS CRADLED
ITER  CADS  ONA
THEDOUGHNUTISAT
OED  CREE  RETE
FLATTEN ANTARES
   RAT SPORE
AMMAN SATIE ASP
LEASTDIGESTIBLE
BACH SNARE SLOP
SLEY MONAD TEES
```

60

```
RELIC JARS ABCD
AMISH AVOW MARE
MEDIO IOTA ONEA
AUSTRALIANCRAWL
   USSR EYELET
MEREST  PER
ETAL ROAR IDEST
RUSSIANROULETTE
VIPER LAWS ARAN
   AMY ARDENT
ERRATA SAGE
CHINESECHECKERS
LOAN TREE ALBEE
ANTA ENNA SEBAT
TEAM REED TESLA
```

61

```
 SUTTER  STAMPS
PENSIVE POPULAR
ARSENAL OREGANO
DIP  NIMROD  CIV
DOE ASCOT  BABE
LUNAR TRIG ITER
ESTEEM EVANGEL
   RCAF EMIT
THIAMIN STOOPS
CREE ALAR TEXAN
LESS  ITALY OLA
AMS ARGOSY  NER
ROISTER URALITE
ALAMODE REHEATS
ONSIDE  ESSENE
```

62

```
SAMP LUMP SABIN
ANOA ALIA PLUTO
BILL BURR OARED
ALEPPO OTIOSE
   ARS IRK AIT
SLIER PACA JUNO
PIMAS ERIN ECTO
INPRINCIPIOERAT
KEEN ETAL SPAKE
ERRS VANE ASTER
SSA DEC  SAG
 TAURUS VERBUM
BLIND LYRE ARNO
LEVEE ANON SITS
TIERS REDS AMOS
```

63

```
PAPAL  MATE  MUG
AZURE CAIRA AXE
CORKDOUGLAS YON
FVE BIBI LENORE
  DYIAN  ELIZ
HAKE NOPE NETS
OMELET TUCKEDIN
FORADAY PARTONE
FORWARDS RAINER
ANYA ASTA EGAD
  GRAF OMITS
DOREMI RICH OGO
AVA ARMAGHEDDON
ZEN IMAGO DAIRY
ENT NAPE ANNEX
```

64

```
BOOR APODAL KAT
BLUE FATIMA ARI
LETSFLYAWAY BEG
 GOOEY RAND ONE
  FLA WUNDERBAR
COTERIE  SANE
APO EDIE  EFOR
SEW DARNHOT ELI
ANNA  DODO  NEO
  SAWS CAMPCOT
RIDINHIGH  ARE
ERR GAEA STAMP
BAA ITSDELOVELY
ETC NOTINA DIOR
LEO ANADEM ANTS
```

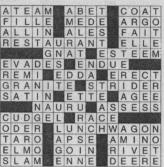
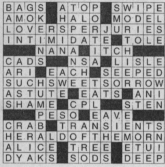

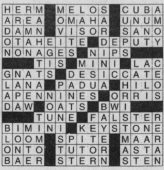

71

```
A V O N   B A B Y   B O Z O
M I C A   E R O O   S I N E W
I C A T C H I N G   C R E E L
G A L O R E   E A S E D
O R A   Y S E R   U N S U N G
    H U T S   S E E I T O I
J A L A P   C L O D   V I T A
U N I V   W H O L E   I C O N
R I C E   H E X A   M E A N T
I S H A D O W   C H A W
S E I N E R   W E A R   T I M
    I G L O O   P I E R R E
S O L F A   K E E P A N I O N
A D I O S   L I M E   S A N S
P E E R   A S S N   E L S A
```

72

```
A A R P   B O H E A   S T E W
H U E R   E N O L S   L O L A
O R N E   H E M O S T A T I C
L I T T L E B O P E E P
A N A T O M Y   E T A   M O A
H O L Y B O O K     M A R Y
    P A T N A   T R I T O N
    M O T H E R G O O S E
S W A L E S   A L O S S
H E I L     S A L T M E A T
Y E N   C A A   S C R U N C H
    B O B B Y S H A F T O E
P E A U D E S O I E   F I R M
A M I N   T I G E S   E R N E
C U R T   S T A R T   T E S S
```

73

```
A M A H   T A L E S   A R E
L O L A   A D O R E   B E T E
B L A I R H O U S E   A P T S
S T E R E O   D E M O C R A T
    L E E S   S P U E
R I G I D   H S T   A S S E S
A N O N   R A C H E L   E V E
P A V E   O P E R A   S N A P
I N E   K E E N E R   I T S A
D E R M A   D E E   E D S E L
    N A R D   S A G E
C A M P A I G N   M A R I A S
P R E P   P R E S I D E N T S
A N N E   L A V E S   A D I T
  E T D   O M E N S   L O S S
```

74

```
S C A R   C A B O   O C H E R
K A L E   O L A S   S H I R E
I F A M A N B I T E S A D O G
D E S I C C A T E D   N E S T
      N E E   N E A T
B R A D   R A N D   L E A S E
R O T   A T L I   F A U L T S
A B O W L O F C H E R R I E S
S O L I D S   H E L M   B E E
S T E L E   S E L L   A I L S
      D R I P   A P T
A L E F   C A L I P E R I N G
P O L I T I C A L A N I M A L
S P I R E   E V E R   S A M E
E S S E N   R E S T   K N E E
```

75

```
B O C A   C A P R I   R S V P
A S A P   O L E A N   E M I R
S T R A P P A R T S   P A S O
S E P T E T   S P E A R E D
    I R E N E   E R S T
P A S T U R E D   C A S T R O
E T T E   W O R T S   R I A
R I O   P R E M I S E   A L S
I M P   R E L I C   M M L I
L E S S O N   T E A R O S E S
    S T U D   E S T A R
I M P E D E D   T I D I N G
V I O L   R E G A L L A G E R
A L T A   E L I S E   N O V A
N O S E   R I N S E   T R A Y
```

76

```
S L A G   A S P E N   B R A T
I O T A   S T O L E   R E N E
P R E S S C O N F E R E N C E
S E E   P E R E   D E A D E N
      W I N E   A L A S
S C A R E D   E L E C T R I C
C A R E S   F L A S H   A D O
A M I N   H A I R S   E D I E
L E E   H A R D Y   B R O O D
A L L I A N C E   S A I N T S
      R U D E   E N N E
R E M I T S   S T E T   S T S
S T A T E O F T H E U N I O N
T A T I   M O L A R   A L G A
U L E S   E B O N Y   B O O P
```

215

77

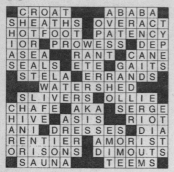

```
C R O A T ▮ ▮ ▮ A B A B A
S H E A T H S ▮ O V E R A C T
H O T F O O T ▮ P A T E N C Y
I O R ▮ P R O W E S S ▮ D E P
A S E A ▮ ▮ R A N T ▮ C A N E
S E A L S ▮ E T E ▮ G A I T S
▮ S T E L A ▮ E R R A N D S ▮
▮ ▮ W A T E R S H E D ▮ ▮ ▮
▮ S L I V E R S ▮ O L L I E ▮
C H A F E ▮ A K A ▮ S E R G E
H I V E ▮ A S I S ▮ R I O T
A N I ▮ D R E S S E S ▮ D I A
R E N T I E R ▮ A M O R I S T
O R I S O N S ▮ D I M O U T S
S A U N A ▮ ▮ ▮ T E E M S
```

78

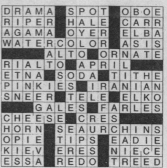

```
D R A M A ▮ S P O T ▮ O B O E
R I P E R ▮ H A L E ▮ C A R R
A G A M A ▮ O Y E R ▮ E L B A
W A T E R C O L O R ▮ A S I S
▮ ▮ ▮ A L T O ▮ O R N A T E
R I A L T O ▮ A P R I L ▮ ▮
E T N A ▮ S O D A ▮ T I T H E
P I N K I E S ▮ I R A N I A N
S N E E R ▮ T E L E ▮ E L K O
▮ ▮ G A L E S ▮ F A R L E S
C H E E S E ▮ C R E S ▮ ▮ ▮
H O R N ▮ S E A U R C H I N S
O P I E ▮ T I P S ▮ E A D I E
K I E V ▮ E R E S ▮ N I E C E
E S S A ▮ R E D O ▮ T R E E D
```

79

```
P O P S ▮ O S A G E ▮ M I S T
A L O E ▮ L E N I N ▮ A N T A
L E O N ▮ E I D E R ▮ N E E R
M A H O G A N Y ▮ A L D E R S
▮ ▮ ▮ R E N E ▮ A G A R ▮ ▮
R E T A R D ▮ P R E T E N S E
E V E ▮ M E R L E ▮ E L A N D
M A S H ▮ R E A T A ▮ S H A G
I D L E S ▮ A N E N T ▮ U K E
T E A M W O R K ▮ T H A M E S
▮ ▮ L A R S ▮ S E A R ▮ ▮ ▮
A L M O N D ▮ A M A R I L L O
H A E C ▮ E L I O T ▮ S U E T
O M S K ▮ R E N T E ▮ E T A T
Y E A S ▮ S A U E R ▮ N E R O
```

80

```
C A R P ▮ C H A T ▮ M A S T S
O V E R ▮ O U L U ▮ A L P E S
N E M O ▮ U N I T ▮ G I A N T
G R O V E R S C O R N E R S ▮
O T T E R S ▮ E R N E ▮ E P I
▮ ▮ S E D G E S ▮ S T A T E D
▮ ▮ ▮ O D I S T ▮ T H E E ▮
S L E P T ▮ N A R ▮ L E E D S
▮ H O N E ▮ E M I L E ▮ ▮ ▮
E N D R I N ▮ S O N A T A ▮ ▮
A G E ▮ N I C E ▮ G A L E N A
▮ J A C K S O N S I S L A N D
L O R R E ▮ L A I C ▮ U S E D
S H E E R ▮ I T S A ▮ D E A L
A N D E S ▮ C E I L ▮ E L L E
```

81

```
R E C A P ▮ T A T A ▮ I G E T
E R O S E ▮ A D E N ▮ S O D A
S I M O N ▮ L A N D P O W E R
T E E N A G E R S ▮ A L I N E
▮ ▮ I G L U ▮ E C L A T ▮ ▮
I G N I T I O N ▮ A S T H M A
B I T S Y ▮ N E A R ▮ E O A N
S R O ▮ C E A S E ▮ U R E
E L O N ▮ A R T E ▮ G E T I N
N I N E T Y ▮ H A R A S S E D
▮ ▮ E R A S E ▮ A L T A ▮ ▮
U P S E T ▮ M I S P L A Y E D
C R O I S S A N T ▮ A T I V E
L A W D ▮ R I T A ▮ T E N O R
A Y N S ▮ A L O T ▮ E D G E R
```

82

```
A L L A H ▮ S C A P E ▮ C C C
D I A N A ▮ T O R E N ▮ H A H
O L D G R A Y H E A D ▮ E L A
S T Y L U S ▮ O N T O ▮ E L I
▮ ▮ ▮ I M P A R T ▮ F A K I R
I D E A ▮ E D T ▮ T R O T S
M U Y ▮ F R E S H ▮ I N F
P O E T I S A ▮ A M M E T E R
▮ S I R ▮ F A R O E ▮ A D E
S C O N E ▮ T E R ▮ S N O B
L O F T S ▮ A T M O S T ▮ ▮ ▮
E B B ▮ A S S E ▮ S T E E L E
E R L ▮ L I P S W E R E R E D
T A U ▮ E N A T E ▮ I R A D E
S S E ▮ S E N S E ▮ A S T A R
```

83

A	D	V		A	N	T	A	L		B	R	A	S
D	O	O	M		L	O	R	R	E		R	O	T	O
A	N	N	A		G	E	O	R	G	S	O	L	T	I
M	A	K	E	F	A	S	T		E	U	G	E	N	E
		A	S	H	E			G	R	A	U			
A	O	R	T	A		B	S	O		V	E	R	S	A
C	Z	A	R		D	A	N	U	B	E		O	L	D
T	A	J	O		S	T	A	G	E		A	B	A	D
E	W	A		S	C	O	R	E	D		R	E	V	E
D	A	N	S	E		N	E	D		S	T	R	A	D
			E	V	A	S			S	H	U	T		
A	D	O	R	E	D		P	E	T	E	R	S	O	N
Z	U	B	I	N	M	E	H	T	A		O	H	I	O
A	N	O	A		A	M	I	T	Y		S	A	L	T
N	E	E	L		N	I	L	E	S			W	Y	E

84

	T	A	P	E	D		H	A	I	T	I	
	B	E	L	A	T	E		U	L	T	I	M	O
A	R	A	B	I	A	N		N	E	C	T	A	R	S
D	U	P	E	D		A	M	T		H	O	G	A	N
Z	I	O	N		S	T	I	E	S		S	I	T	A
E	S	T		S	T	U	A	R	T	S		N	O	G
D	E	S	P	A	I	R	S		O	T	T	E	R	S
			H	O	P	E		P	R	O	A			
S	A	B	I	N	E		C	L	E	A	N	E	R	S
E	R	R		E	N	D	E	A	R	S		L	O	T
P	E	O	N		D	E	N	T	S		B	A	D	E
A	N	N	A	S		S	A	T		M	A	T	E	R
L	A	C	T	O	S	E		E	R	O	S	I	O	N
	S	O	A	R	E	R		R	A	T	I	O	S	
	S	L	A	N	T		S	H	E	E	N			

85

T	I	D	E		A	B	E	T		N	U	M	B
U	V	E	A		F	L	O	R	A		A	T	O	I
T	E	S	T		A	L	A	R	K		S	A	U	R
U	S	C		S	L	I	T		E	T	C	H	E	D
			E	L	U	L		O	S	H	A			
A	B	N	E	R	S		P	E	T	E	R	S	O	N
N	O	D	O	F	F		A	S	H	Y		T	A	E
O	R	A	N		R	A	N	E	E		P	U	R	E
D	A	N		R	O	P	E		P	L	U	M	E	D
E	X	T	R	E	M	E	S		L	A	M	B	D	A
			I	N	G	S		U	R	A	L			
S	O	L	V	E	R		H	A	N	D		E	C	U
O	K	I	E		A	L	O	N	G		A	B	A	S
F	A	R	R		C	U	R	I	E		L	U	T	E
A	Y	E	S		E	V	A	S		A	M	O	S	

86

M	A	S	S	E		D	A	S	H		H	A	R	K
A	N	N	E	S		I	N	T	O		O	P	A	L
S	T	O	A	T		N	O	A	H		N	I	N	E
H	I	B	B	I	N	G		L	U	G	G	A	G	E
			A	V	I	D			A	M	O	K		
S	I	N	G	A	L	O	N	G		B	O	N	U	S
I	S	O		L	E	N	A		S	N	A	R	L	
G	L	O	W		G	N	P		G	O	B	I		
M	A	N	I	A		K	I	E	V		M	A	N	
A	M	E	N	D		T	I	N	G	A	L	I	N	G
			G	E	N	E		G	E	R	E			
G	A	R	D	N	E	R		P	R	I	N	C	E	S
O	N	E	I		P	E	P	O		A	D	O	R	E
S	P	I	N		A	S	I	N		N	E	V	I	N
H	A	N	G		L	A	N	G		T	R	E	N	D

87

	S	C	A	D		A	D	I	M		T	R	A	P
C	E	A	S	E		B	I	L	E		H	O	B	O
A	L	L	I	N		E	V	E	S		E	B	O	N
B	L	I	N	D	F	A	I	T	H		M	O	D	E
			R	A	M	S		E	M	O	T	E	S	
E	D	I	T	O	R		O	L	D	E	N			
D	I	S	H		C	A	R	E		A	K	I	M	
D	E	L	E	T	E	D		S	E	N	E	G	A	L
	S	E	R	E		E	D	E	N		E	E	R	Y
			A	L	E	N	E		T	A	S	T	E	S
L	E	S	S	E	N		N	O	R	M				
E	R	I	C		M	O	O	D	Y	B	L	U	E	S
A	N	D	A		E	T	T	E		L	O	R	N	A
S	I	L	L		S	T	E	T		E	R	G	O	T
T	E	E	S		H	O	D	S		R	E	E	L	

88

	F	E	T	E	S			D	I	N	A	R	
D	E	V	I	L	E	D		S	A	T	I	N	E	T
E	M	I	R	A	T	E		P	H	E	L	A	I	E
C	A	D		M	U	L	L	I	N	S		T	A	P
A	L	E	S		P	A	I	R	S		P	O	R	E
L	E	N	T	O		Y	E	E		W	I	L	D	E
	S	T	A	C	K	S		S	P	A	R	E	S	
			S	H	E				E	R	A			
	A	T	H	E	N	S		C	A	N	T	E	R	
S	N	E	E	R		T	E	A		S	E	R	E	S
T	E	N	D		C	A	R	V	E		D	A	T	A
E	S	T		T	U	R	N	I	P	S		S	I	B
E	T	A	G	E	R	E		L	E	I	S	U	R	E
N	O	G	A	L	E	S		S	E	V	E	R	E	R
	F	E	L	L	S			S	A	W	E	D		

89

A	H	A	B		H	I	S	S		M	I	F	F	S
S	A	T	I		E	D	I	E		I	N	L	E	T
P	R	O	A		R	E	A	R		S	T	O	R	E
		I	M	F	R	O	M	M	I	S	S	O	U	R	I
	R	O	I			E	P	I			T	O	N	
A	G	R	A	I	N	O	F	S	A	L	T			
R	I	O		L	E	N	O			E	A	G	L	E
I	S	L	E		S	E	R	R	A		G	R	A	Y
A	T	L	A	S			T	I	N	T		I	K	E
	T	O	T	H	E	M	A	R	I	N	E	S		
A	C	T		F	R	A			P	I	N			
D	O	U	B	T	I	N	G	T	H	O	M	A	S	
A	B	B	I	E		N	A	S	O		A	L	O	E
M	O	A	T	S		A	L	A	R		T	A	N	K
S	L	E	E	T		H	E	R	A		E	S	S	E

90

D	E	M	I		C	A	R	T	A		O	L	A	V
E	L	A	N		O	C	E	A	N		D	O	G	E
B	I	N	S		L	O	Q	U	A	C	I	O	U	S
T	O	N	I		D	R	U		D	O	C	K	E	T
S	T	E	T	S		N	I	C	E	R				
		Q	U	I	P		R	E	M	A	R	Q	U	E
T	C	U		P	I	P	E	R			P	U	G	S
E	R	I	C		E	L	D	E	R		M	E	L	T
R	E	N	O		A	R	S	O	N		E	Y	E	
M	E	S	Q	U	I	T	E		B	O	S	N		
			S	N	E	A	D		G	N	O	M	E	
T	A	B	L	E	S		D	E	B		A	L	A	W
S	Q	U	A	R	E	M	I	L	E		R	I	F	E
A	U	N	T		C	A	N	T	S		E	V	I	L
R	A	K	E		T	O	G	A	S		D	E	A	L

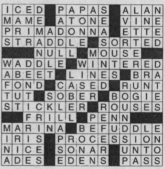

91

J	U	D	O		F	R	I	S	K		Q	U	A	Y
A	S	O	N		A	N	N	I	E		U	N	T	O
R	E	C	E	P	T	A	C	L	E		A	D	A	Y
		O	R	O		A	L	P	A	C	I	N	O	
S	I	G	N	O	F	F		A	R	K	S			
A	M	O	O	D		A	B	A	F	T		G	U	R
S	P	U	N		F	R	O	S	T	Y		U	N	E
H	O	P	E		O	R	O	S	E		H	I	R	T
A	S	A		B	R	A	Z	E	R		A	S	E	A
Y	E	N		O	C	H	E	R		C	R	E	A	K
			D	O	Z	E			T	W	A	D	D	L	E
G	A	D	Z	O	O	K	S		A	L	C			
A	T	O	Z		P	A	P	E	R	M	O	N	E	Y
R	O	W	I		E	V	A	D	E		R	I	L	E
E	R	N	E		N	A	M	E	S		E	X	I	T

92

I	C	E	D		P	A	P	A	S		A	L	A	N
M	A	M	E		A	T	O	N	E		V	I	N	E
P	R	I	M	A	D	O	N	N	A		E	T	T	E
S	T	R	A	D	D	L	E		S	O	R	T	E	D
			N	U	L	L		M	O	U	S	E		
W	A	D	D	L	E		W	I	N	T	E	R	E	D
A	B	E	E	T		L	I	N	E	S		B	R	A
F	O	N	D		C	A	S	E	D		R	U	N	T
T	U	T		S	O	B	E	R		B	O	G	I	E
S	T	I	C	K	L	E	R		R	O	U	S	E	S
		F	R	I	L	L		P	E	N	N			
M	A	R	I	N	A		B	E	F	U	D	D	L	E
I	R	I	S		P	R	O	C	E	S	S	I	O	N
N	I	C	E		S	O	N	A	R		U	N	T	O
A	D	E	S		E	D	E	N	S		P	A	S	S

93

H	O	H	O		D	A	L	E			S	P	A
A	M	A	T		B	O	N	E	S		H	E	R	R
Y	O	W	T	H	E	Y	G	O	T	M	E	P	A	L
S	O	N		A	G	E	E			O	R	A	T	E
		T	W	I	N			C	U	D	D	L	E	S
P	A	D	U	A	N		C	A	N	E	S			
A	L	I	B	I		S	A	R	I		A	P	E	
D	O	E	S	I	T	H	U	R	T	A	W	F	U	L
S	E	T			R	O	S	Y		N	O	R	M	A
			S	M	I	T	E		S	T	R	O	P	S
M	O	S	L	E	M	S		A	C	H	E			
A	R	E	A	S			I	R	A	E		O	R	B
N	A	W	T	H	E	Y	G	O	T	M	E	P	A	L
E	N	E	S		T	R	E	S	S		L	A	T	E
S	T	R			E	S	T	E			F	L	E	W

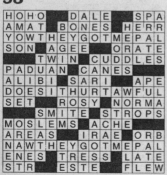

94

D	I	E	S		S	M	E	W			L	A	P
I	R	A	E		P	A	R	A	D	E		E	M	U
N	E	S	T		A	D	D	L	E	D		O	A	R
A	N	Y	T	I	M	E		T	W	O	B	I	T	S
H	E	M	E	N		O	R	E		M	O	X	I	E
			O	R	C		V	E	R	M	I	N		
W	E	N	S		B	E	D		I	T	A	L	I	A
E	V	E		P	E	R	C	A	L	E		A	C	E
B	A	Y	A	R	D		E	U	S		V	U	E	S
			D	O	E	S	N	T		H	A	N		
P	R	O	U	D		I	T	O		I	N	D	I	A
S	A	W	B	U	C	K		M	A	S	T	E	R	S
A	L	L		C	L	A	R	A	S		A	R	A	S
L	E	E		T	E	N	E	T	S		G	E	N	E
M	S	T			G	O	A	T			E	D	I	T

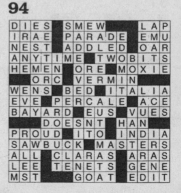

```
S A M E . A D D S . R E D A S
E R A S . P R O T . A M O L E
L I L T . P A N E . G E E S E
F L E E C E G A T E O R R O D
. . . L A S . . M U G . . .
L A S C A R . P R O T E S T S
A N E A R . S E A T . . A R I
D O L L A R W A R E O R F O X
E L L . E A S E . S I E V E
D E S O L A T E . S C O R E S
. . S I C . . P T A . .
P L A T E T Y P E O R F O I L
R O G E R . O R A L . A N T I
O C E A N . R O L E . S C A N
S I D L E . E D E N . T E L E
```

```
P O O F . S C A R F . Q U I P
E N D O . T A C H O . U N T O
A C E R . E S T E R . A I L S
Y E R T L E T H E T U R T L E
. . . U E L E . . R S T . .
A R E N A S . O P E C . B A N
C O L A S . D A I S . M A R E
H A S T E M A K E S W A S T E
E R I E . O V E R . A C T E D
S S E . E D E N . L I K E L Y
. . A L E . . D A T E . .
D E N N I S T H E M E N A C E
E L O N . T R I B E . Z I O N
J U N E . L E T T S . I N A T
A L E X . Y E A S T . E T T E
```

```
R E B E C . A M A H . I N C A
E R A T O . S O D A . N E A L
E N D O W . T A I L . T O I L
L I L . P R E T T Y P E N N Y
S E Y M O U R . . A I R . .
. . A K I N G S R A N S O M
S I L K E N . R I D . O D A
A R I E S . B A T . S P A I N
G A M . S U N . S T E R N E
O N E A S Y S T R E E T . .
. . . G A S . O A R S M A N
M O N E Y T O B U R N . O L E
A G I O . O M I T . U N I T E
S E L L . L A N E . M I R E D
H E E D . E N D S . S P A R S
```

```
. T A B . A B B Y . M I N E
A R L O . N I L E . M I L E R
D A V Y J O N E S . I C I E R
A L I D A D E S . E S K E R S
M A N . D I S T A S T E . .
. . . R E Z . . S P R Y E R
A L T I . E M I T . A F T E R
N I E C E . O D E . L I T E R
A M A H S . N O R M . N E D S
P R A T E D . A R N . . .
. . R E N O V A T E . T R I
P A D D E D . I N A N D O U T
A L A R M . J O E D O A K E S
T O D O S . A I L O . L E D A
E P E E . B A E R . I N E .
```

```
A B A . . B E T T E . F E E S
G U L P . A C H E D . A M A T
O R E L . T R A N S . M I T E
G R E Y H O U N D . O I L F R
. . M I N S K . A R L E N E
D E V O N . S O R R Y . .
A L E U T . O G R E . R E A P
M I N T . A D I N A . E R D A
P A T H . L O V E . L U M E N
. . C A P R I . I N A N E . .
L E M O N S . N A O M I . .
E X U L T . A G R O N O M I C
O T R O . A L D E N . N O V A
R O A N . P L A T A . S O A K
A L L Y . H A Y E S . N N E
```

```
R A S P S . C H A R . S K A T
A S I A N . P O L O . T I N E
H O R N E D O W L S . A N T S
. R E N E W . E Y E S I G H T
. . I R I S . . T U R F . .
R O S E . N E G A T E . I R E
O M A R . E L A T E D . S E R
M A N S E . D U B . E T H A N
A N D . A P O G E E . R E T E
N I P . T A M E S T . I R A S
. . I T E R . . T U L A . .
A M P E R A G E . D E N S E
T O E S . B A L D E A G L E S
T O R T . L O B E . S L U G S
U R S A . E L A N . T E R S E
```